THE ATLANTIC CRITICAL REVIEW

QUARTERLY

A Peer Reviewed Journal Indexed in
MLA Directory of Periodicals

JANUARY – JUNE 2015

VOLUME 14 NUMBERS 1-2

ATLANTIC

PUBLISHERS & DISTRIBUTORS (P) LTD

CONTRIBUTORS

Saikat Sarkar, Assistant Professor, Department of English (PG & UG), Bankura Christian College, Bankura-722101, West Bengal.

J.S. Kirubahar, Associate Professor of English, VHNSN College (Autonomous), Virudhunagar-626001, Tamil Nadu.

K.S. Balaji, teaches English at the Language Centre, Sultan Qatoos University, the Sultanate of Oman.

Averi Mukhopadhyay, Research Scholar, Department of Humanities and Social Sciences, IIT Roorkee, Uttarakhand-247667.

Rashmi Gaur, Professor, Department of Humanities and Social Sciences, IIT Roorkee, Uttarakhand-247667.

Ramona L. Ceciu, Researcher, Department of Comparative Literature, Jadavpur University, Kolkata-700032.

Vera Shamina, Professor, Department of Philology, Kazan State University, Kazan, Russia; [R] Shkolnii pereulok d.2, kv.57, 420012 Kazan.

Rama Kundu, Former UGC Emeritus Fellow (2013-2015); Former Professor of English, Burdwan University, Burdwan-713104, West Bengal.

THE ATLANTIC CRITICAL REVIEW
VOLUME 14 NUMBERS 1-2 (JANUARY-JUNE 2015)

CONTENTS

Biblical Names and Figures in the Later Novels of Toni Morrison: Affinities with and Departure from the Source

SAIKAT SARKAR

The act of naming is the great and solemn consolation of mankind.
—Elias Canetti (*The Agony of Flies*)

TONI Morrison's fictional oeuvre reflects an ambivalence arising out of her fascination and critical attitude towards the *Bible*. This mixed response of Morrison towards the Holy Book makes her fictional repertoire a complex site of conflicting images, myths and ideas. That her fiction is replete with traces of her ancestral African culture is well acknowledged by critics. But her allegiance to her African-American identity does not make her ignore the impact of Christianity on the black Americans. Though Christianity and its scripture were forcibly imposed on the slaves to deprive them of their original identities, years of living with it have made it a part of their lives and culture. Morrison's ambivalent stance towards the *Bible* stems from this complex tradition.

An astute reader of Morrison can trace a biblical nomenclature behind the names of the bulk of Morrison's characters. Regarding *Song of Solomon,* she observed in an interview: "I used the biblical names to show the impact of the Bible on the lives of black people, their awe of and respect for it coupled with their ability to distort it for their own purposes" (LeClair 126). This observation applies not only to *Song of Solomon*, but also to her whole fictional repertoire. Morrison's selection of biblical names is anything but random. Significantly, the personae bearing the names usually serve to highlight and underscore deviations from—rather than semblance with—their namesakes in the source. There are instances of distortion, inversion, departure, and variation in Morrison's use of biblical names for her characters. Also, there are occasions when she would simultaneously subvert and exploit the significance and associations that are conventionally attached to a biblical character, in order to highlight the condition of a black man/woman in the white-centric world. Examples abound in her novels.

Though Toni Morrison established her practice of making ambivalent use of biblical names in her very first novel, *The Bluest Eye*, and continued doing so in *Sula* and *Song of Solomon,* this paper will focus on her strategic use of biblical names for her characters in her later novels, namely *Tar Baby* (1981), *Beloved* (1987), *Paradise* (1997) and *A Mercy* (2008). Though Morrison two more novels (*Jazz* and *Love*) between *Tar Baby* and *A Mercy* and one (*Home*) afterwards, in this paper I will leave them out of the ambit of discussion. The reason for doing so is that though even in these novels Morrison's use of biblical names can be traced her use of such is not extensive. The four later novels under discussion are replete with strong biblical undercurrents manifested through her use of various biblical myths and elements. Even more conspicuous is her use of biblical names which posits to her novels an angularity and reflects faithfully the ambivalent relation the blacks have with the Bible and the white culture it represents.

The fourth novel in Morrison's oeuvre, *Tar Baby* (1981) has a classic colonial schema at the center of it. Valerian Street, a self-exiled candy merchant, lords over a house by maintaining a hierarchy of positions for his servants. His wife Margaret is unhappy with life and his foster child Jadine, who is actually a niece to Valerian's servants Sydney and Ondine, aims to make it big in the fashion world. The novel records how things change with the arrival of an outsider, Son, who brings redemptive possibilities especially for Jadine. Interestingly, Valerian has named his house 'L'Arbe de la Croix' (*Tar Baby* 52) which could be translated as 'the cross of Christ'. In Christian theology, the 'cross' not only signifies an instrument of torture but also a burden that one has to undertake. The character that Morrison entrusts with the responsibility of carrying the burden of bringing the message of redemption for Jadine is aptly named Son. This reinforces a connection between him and the title 'Son of Man' used interchangeably for Jesus in the 'New Testament' (Matthew 10:32, Mark 8:38). It is possible to connect Son also with Moses, the harbinger of redemption in the 'Old Testament'. Moses was also a foster 'son' of the Pharaoh. Like Moses, Son also plays the role of a guide to entangled ones. However, Son's portrayal is not mono-dimensional, as he, unlike Moses, stands in need to be redeemed himself at the end of the novel.

The characters in *Tar Baby* re-enact the basic situation of those who lived in biblical paradise, as they live in a realm of innocence. This innocence is an incomplete, even strategic one. Oblivious to what is happening outside and unwilling to take risks the characters live cocooned in their carefully crafted existence. The arrival of Son signals changes. As he initiates changes and thus disturbs the settled order, he can be compared to the biblical serpent, the eternal tempter who provoked Eve to rebel and thereby led to their banishment from paradise. In his essay "The Crime of Innocence: *Tar Baby* and the Fall Myth", Terry Otten compares Son with the serpent. Otten describes Son as the "serpent in paradise…a distinctly black outlaw, a fugitive who…first appears at night, emerging from the waters of the unconscious self" (44). But the situation seems to point at significance beyond this reductive formulation where Valerian can be unquestionably equated with God. Neither can Son be categorized as the serpent in a conclusive way. Son can be indeed envisioned as the Christ figure as well. His name also suggests that. Otten further contends in the essay:

> More than the conventional tempter in the garden, Son is the manifestation of the black pariah in Western culture, the terrorizing black male, the supposed rapist of the white women…Son becomes something of a parody of the Christ figure.… Like the suffering Christ figure who brings redemption, Son is rejected by those he possesses the power to transform. (44-45)

The novel remains inconclusive regarding the issue of redemption; whether Son brings redemption for Jadine, or he himself stands in need for one.

Parallels, however, can be drawn between Son and Christ. Just like Christ who is the be-all and end-all of the gospels, *Tar Baby* begins and ends with Son. Morrison evokes a gamut of allusions. She likens Son's hair to 'foliage' which 'from a distance…looked like…the crown of a deciduous tree' (*Tar Baby* 132). The tree imagery recalls the cross of Christ. The name of Son's hometown Eloe sounds very similar to Eloi which means God. Interestingly, Jesus cries 'Eloi' from the cross. Son's transformation from a swamp nigger to a clean and attractive black man recalls Jesus' transfiguration (Mark 9:3). Like Jesus who "did not come to bring peace, but a sword" (Matthew 10:34), Son is not out there to have a peaceful time either as he intrudes to encourage everyone's return to his or her true self. And much like Jesus whose influence was felt by all and sundry, Son's arrival also ushers in the stir of life in

L'Arbe de la Croix. Again, in an alternative reading, Son can be looked at as a variant of the trickster figure. The title of the novel lends itself to such a reading. He can be read as the Br'er Rabbit and Jadine can be identified with the 'tar baby' of the tale. However, in his ability to bring redemption and his rejection at the hands of those for whom he brings such possibilities Son can very well be read as a variation of the Christ figure. At the same time he can also be read as a variation of the serpent as well. Morrison, in the character of Son, revises the traditional association of the words 'Son of Man' fusing into him both the attributes of Christ and the serpent. She, thereby, seems to reject a divisive either/or attitude endorsed by the Western theology and advocates an inclusive worldview which is enriched by layers of meaning. The novel ends on an ambiguous note as Jadine goes back to the glittering world of fashion and Son heads towards the mythical horsemen who inhabit the island and who can bring redemption for Son by connecting him to his cultural past. Morrison resists conclusive reading and in a reversal of the tale puts Son (the Christ figure) in a situation where he himself would be in need of redemption.

The ambivalent portrayal of Son in which he can both be seen as Christ figure and the serpent calls back to mind the ingenious story "The Three Versions of Judas" written by Jorge Luis Borges. In this story, written in the form of an article, Borges works upon the discoveries by a fictitious writer Nils Runeberg and puts forward three formulations. First is that Judas is the human counterpart of Jesus. Second is that Judas is the extreme ascetic. Borges writes: "The ascetic, for the greater glory of God, degrades and mortifies the flesh; Judas did the same with the spirit. He renounced honor, good, peace, the Kingdom of Heaven, as others, less heroically, renounced pleasure" (Borges 154). His third formulation is that Judas is the real incarnation of God, and that he willingly chose to sacrifice his spirit so that Jesus may sacrifice his flesh to earn redemption. Such an ingenious reading (Borges, however, substantiates his arguments with textual references) questions the settled and traditional beliefs and makes it possible for the reader to decipher alternative meanings of the scripture. Morrison's Son with his ambivalence questions order and brings in the scope to arrive at alternative meanings.

The surname Childs can be connected with biblical concept of children. In the 'New Testament' Christians are sometimes addressed as 'children' (Galatians 4:19), a practice associated with Jesus (John 21:5). They refer to themselves as 'children of God' (Romans 8:16) to denote the special relationship with God which they have inherited as the people of the new 'covenant'. Jadine's surname suggests ironic undertones as she is hardly a child of her ancestral culture. She has molded herself according to the Western white sensibilities and standards of beauty. Successful in the white world, Jadine is contemptuous of her own people and thus presents a contrast to Frances Harper's Iola Leroy. Having been rescued by the Union soldiers from slavery, Iola has the option of passing for a white woman at the end of the Civil War. But she opts for her racial identity. Harper wanted an intellectual elite class who would be committed to the cause of race. Jadine, riding on her Western upbringing, does exactly the opposite. Son sees through Jadine's constructed identity and deflates her pride in her education: "...you don't know anything, anything at all about your children and anything at all about your mama and your papa..." (*Tar Baby* 267). Son rekindles in her the memory of shame she felt at the sight of a black woman in a Paris street who was proud of her heritage.

Son led her to a new birth as he "unorphaned her completely. Gave her a brand-new childhood" (*Tar Baby* 231). But her lack of connection with her uncle and aunt and her self-constructed paradise is not a fitting place for Son to live in and he takes her to his lost Eden in Eloe. But she can't live there either. Startled by a vision of a host of black women who condemn her, she flees Eloe. These night women are the racial ghosts who demand from her recognition of her racial identity. Her final choice to go back to her white world of fashion cannot be easily dismissed as something negative. If on the one hand, she rejects her cultural roots in order to embrace a foreign ideal, on the other hand, she affirms her freedom by rejecting to live subservient to Son. Torn between her racial and sexual location Jadine remains a true child to her own self. Otten aptly summarizes her final position "Jadine's 'fall' leads to no regeneration. Cast east of Eden she exists in unresolved duality, knowing 'good' and 'evil', black and white" (Otten, "*Tar Baby* and the Fall Myth" 49).

Sydney and Ondine, who bear the same surname, are also guilty of not being true children to their cultural locations either. Proud of their servile positions in a white household, they even call fellow blacks Gideon and Therese by their generic names; Yardman and one of the Maries. They are contemptuous of Son and look down upon him as an aberration. Interestingly, Therese, who is called one of the Maries, guides Son to his true goal and helps to make the right choice when he is split between his desire to follow Jadine and his wish to embrace the mythical horsemen, his cultural ancestors. In this the naming is evocative, as like the biblical Mary (though the *Bible* mentions seven Maries, it is apt to analogize Therese with Virgin Mary) he guides Son (the Christ figure) to his destiny. The son of Valerian and Margaret is also fittingly named Michael. Michael is mentioned by Jude in his epistle as an accuser who disputes with the Devil, but who is apparently not very strong or effective reprove: "But even the archangel Michael, when he was disputing with the devil...did not dare to bring a slanderous accusation against him, but said, 'the lord rebuke you'" (Jude 9). In *Tar Baby* also Michael plays an adversarial role in his admonishment of Jadine for embracing a foreign culture while neglecting her own but his influence is not strong on Jadine to make her accept her ancestral culture. *Tar Baby* is structured as a re-situating of a popular folk tale, that of the Br'er Rabbit and the tar baby. However, Morrison's naming of the characters with biblical parallels contextualizes them from a fresh perspective by means of highlighting subtle departures from as well as similarities with the source.

Beloved (1987), one of the very best of Morrison, is definitely the most complex of her novels. Based on a real event, it narrates the striking tale of Sethe Suggs, a slave woman who tried to kill her children to save them from the menace of slavery. She, however, managed to kill only one. Years later she is visited by a young woman who, in the magical realistic narrative, appears to be her dead daughter. The young woman is named Beloved who, it seems is determined to avenge herself on her mother. The novel ends with Sethe's realization of her true self and the community's decision to come in her aid after having outcast her for years. Presented in a layered narrative, the novel is a gripping tale of human relationships as well as an authentic documentation of slavery.

Morrison's choice of name for her protagonist in the novel carries an overt biblical allusion. Seth is the third son of Adam and Eve (Genesis 4:25) and is regarded as heralding a more respectable line than that of Cain. The line of Seth, with its dependence on God, is contrasted with the proud self-reliance of the line of Cain. The *Bible* connotes that the human race is propagated through the line of Seth (Genesis 5:7). Morrison's Sethe, however, is not assigned any such position or role.

On the other hand, it is possible to trace a connection between Sethe and Cain, the brother of her biblical namesake.

The magnitude of Cain's crime, his murder of Abel due to jealousy, is doubled by his refusal to mourn. For this he is branded and then banished to 'wander' about the world. Cain is an early exile, and thus can be connected with the black Americans—all uprooted from their home and homeland. Morrison's Sethe seems to be indeed the opposite of the biblical paradigm. Instead of begetting a glorious and prosperous line she rather seeks to squash all her progenies, though she succeeds in ripping only one. She is neither acclaimed nor valorized, but condemned instead for her strange criminality. Killing one's own children is an appalling act by any cultural standard, but Morrison helps the reader to see the same act from a very different perspective. Sethe's very name suggests an ironical inversion of the response associated with the biblical Seth, and she represents a helpless situation where she has no choice but to kill her own child as an act of desperate love. Sethe is also connected with Cain by the mark she has on her body, a mark etched by the whipping of her eventual owner, Schoolteacher and his two nephews. Though she acts in pure desperation, her murder of her baby girl is not accepted by the community and Sethe, like Cain, becomes outcast.

Sethe's mark, though imprinted by man (not God), suggests ambivalent meanings in the context of her struggle, her act of denial and assertion which become paradoxically interchangeable. Sethe's act of killing her child can be seen as hideous, but it is an act committed in desperate mercy, and, thereby, can be seen as a redemptive act committed by a mother for whom denying life is a lesser evil than the evils of slavery. However, Sethe compounds her crime by not attending the funeral of her mother-in-law Baby Suggs. She is guilty of pride and is seconded in this by her community which also acts in a proud manner and excommunicates her. Both of them are marked. Sethe is in need of 'rememory', a transcreative act that shapes the events of the past into story. Memory has a formative power that helps one to 'disremember' one's unhappy past and places it in proper position. Cain refused to mourn, but Sethe must undergo mourning and recognize memory in order to achieve wholeness.

Sethe's mark looks like a chokeberry tree. Deborah Guth, in her essay "'Wonder what God had in mind': *Beloved*'s Dialogue with Christianity", sees Sethe's mark as having "Christological echoes" and holds that the motif of Christ's Cross and Passion "spans the entire text" of *Beloved* (Guth 87). She further contends that the evocation of the suffering of Christ "characterize[s] the long history of black suffering focused through the story of Sethe" (Guth 87). Sethe can be associated with Christ in her bearing a cross (the tree has often been cited as a symbol of the cross) and the tree-like mark on her back features "roses of blood" (*Beloved* 114) which, Guth contends, "blossoms on her skin like drops from Jesus' brow"; drops that recall the "blood of sacrifice" (Guth 87) that Christ shed for the sins of the world.

Stamp Paid is another character in *Beloved* who has a biblical namesake. Prior to changing his name to Stamp Paid—because he thought he had paid his dues to his master by letting him have his wife—Stamp was originally named Joshua. Joshua, in the 'Old Testament', is chosen by God to succeed Moses as the leader of Israel and is made into a strong and courageous leader. In the post-exilic period, Joshua is an important figure in the tales of 'Exodus', and the subsequent Israelite conquest. A charismatic leader, Joshua declares to his people "choose for yourselves this day whom you will serve…as for me and my household, we will serve the Lord" (Joshua 24:15). God exhorted Joshua to help the people cross the Jordan River. Stamp Paid also rows his boat to ferry the runaway slaves (he transported Sethe) across the river to freedom. He is also a leader of the community in many ways. He saved Denver from being killed by her mother, convinced Baby Suggs to come back to the clearing, and encouraged the community to forgive Sethe and to come to her aid. However, he appears to hold a judgmental 'Old Testament' attitude. The 'Book of Joshua' is about the possession of the Promised Land and the importance of the land for a nomadic group for developing their identity. Ironically, Morrison's story is the story of the dispossessed and the character of Stamp Paid is a sad documentation of the dispossession thrust by slavery.

The name Beloved is taken from the *Bible*. Though the epigraph is taken from the 'Romans', it can be connected to a passage from 'Hosea' as well. The passage reads: "In that day", declares the Lord, "you will call me 'my husband', you will no longer call me 'my master'" (Hosea 2:16). By God's decree Hosea married the prostitute Gomer and the book's reference to God as a husband to a chosen (but presently not loved) wife relates to the situation of the apostate Jews who had lost favour with God. It also relates to Morrison's epigraph to *Beloved*. The novel's reference to an 'Old Testament' marriage between a powerful husband and an un-beloved woman, who becomes a beloved bride, invites a reading of *Beloved* as an allegorical revision of another 'Old Testament' book; 'Song of Songs'. Reconciliation is an important theme of *Beloved* and it is also important to 'Song of Songs' which records the consummation of love between Solomon and his black bride, the Queen of Sheba. The lovers' relationship is traditionally interpreted as a manifestation of the relationship between Christ and his bride, the Church. This 'Old Testament' story has a close relation to the passage from 'Romans' used as the novel's epigraph. The beloved bride of Solomon can be considered an analogy for God's chosen people in the 'New Testament'. Solomon himself is considered to be not only a Jewish king, but also the prophetic representation of Christ and his beloved is not only the Ethiopian Queen of Sheba, but the representation of the beloved bride of Christ.

The figure of a black woman as the bride of Christ is significant. Sondra O'Neale, in "Inhibiting Midwives, Usurping Creators", notes that an early church father, Origen, pointed out that the black woman in the biblical 'Song of Songs' was a symbol of the bride of Christ. She analyses the degradation of black women and contends "through the use of thoroughly pejorative connotations in literature and art created to accommodate the emerging slave trade, black women were presented in societal media as icons of evil rather than examples of divine beauty" (O'Neale 142). Interestingly, Beloved reminds Paul D "of that headless bride back behind Sweet Home" (*Beloved* 13). Beloved being called headless is not unnatural as Sethe tried to slit her throat. But her being called a 'headless bride' lends itself to an allegorical interpretation. In the 'New Testament', the Church is conceived as the body which is separated from its head, Christ. In his epistle to the Ephesians Paul establishes the connection between Christ and the Church as that of between a husband and wife: "For this reason a man will leave his father and mother and be united to his wife and the two will become one flesh. This is a profound mystery—but I am talking about Christ and the church" (Ephesians 5:31-32). Similar metaphors can also be found in John 3:29; Revelations 18:23; 22:17; and 2 Corinthians 11:2. The *Bible* promises that both will be reunited in a celestial marriage supper: "Let us rejoice and be glad and give him glory! For the wedding of the Lamb has come, and his bride has made herself ready" (Revelations 19:7). But despite such a promise of celestial union, the bride, on the earth, is rejected as un-loved. Morrison's Beloved also longs to be united to her loved one as a bride longs to be united with her husband. But she is also rejected and has to leave Sethe at the end of the novel.

The analogy between the realm of Solomon and the situation in the mid-nineteenth century USA can be related together as in the latter one dominant group's ruthless treatment of the people whose 'not beloved' status is very apparent. Solomon's beloved repeatedly says "I am black, but comely" (*Song of Songs* 1:5). The beloved is programmed by a dominant discourse which decrees that one cannot be both black and comely (beautiful) and that a black man/woman's beauty must always be qualified with a 'but'. The daughters of Jerusalem are displeased with Solomon's beloved for she falls short of the socially accepted norm of beauty and portrays a beautiful black woman modeled on the beloved of Solomon. That Beloved is beautiful is admitted by Sethe, Paul D and the women of the society. Morrison's Beloved craves sweets, especially honey (*Beloved* 55), and her "breath was exactly like new milk" (*Beloved* 98). Solomon says to his beloved, "Thy lips...drop as the honeycomb: honey and milk are under your tongue" (*Song of Songs* 4:11).

Morrison's portrayal of Beloved is carefully directed towards evoking a biblical parallel. This is articulated not only in acknowledgement of the influence of a dominant group of people over others, but also in knowledge of the ways which can subvert it. Morrison revises the relationship between the beloved, albeit rejected, black women and those who reject them. Both the texts are connected by a pain of separation from the one who is the object of devoted love. Solomon's beloved laments; "The watchmen that went about the city found me, they smote me, they wounded me" (*Song of Songs* 5:6). Morrison's Beloved is also estranged from the object of love by the schoolteacher and his nephews and the community people. However, it is not only the watchmen who treat the bride in *Song of Songs* with impunity, but the more powerful lover, who could have protected his beloved from such impunity, also withdraws himself inexplicably. The beloved mourns; "I opened to my beloved; but my beloved had withdrawn himself and was gone" (*Song of Songs* 5:6). In both the texts, rejected and abandoned persons are degraded by not only the power, but also by someone who had previously loved and protected them.

Paul D's name comes directly from the *Bible*. A mate of Sethe in the Sweet Home, Paul was sold by the owner and was subjected to a life of prolonged torture. Paul D's life and the suffering he was subjected to bear a testimony to the painful condition of the Black slaves. Three Pauls are mentioned in *Beloved*; Paul A, Paul D and Paul F who are all brothers. Their names imply the presence of Paul B, Paul C and Paul E as well who, we presume, have gone lost. The use of the single name with all these one-letter suffixes also shows how careless the slave-owners were, who did not even take care in individualizing the different Pauls. We gather the information that the owner sells out Paul A and Paul F is hanged. Paul D is also sold out after their escape attempt of escaping fails. He comes back years later to Sethe. Like his biblical counterpart, Paul D turns didactic towards Sethe trying to tell her what should be the right way to love. Again, like the 'New Testament' Paul, Paul D also fights secret afflictions while fighting evil. Paul D keeps a tin box tightly locked up in which he is supposed to have kept his past memories. *Beloved* pries it open and Paul D leaves Sethe's household. Having seen much, and suffered much, he believes that he knows what is right for Sethe, but paradoxically he stands in need of self-realization himself. Through this realization Morrison subverts the image of the biblical Paul who is credited to have formulated Christianity and is supposed to have lived a spotless life. The biblical Paul was converted, and Paul D in *Beloved* also gets converted at the end when he, along with Sethe, realizes that in order to receive wholeness they must go through their past for creating a meaningful today and that they "need some kind of tomorrow" (*Beloved* 273). Like his biblical namesake, Paul D also has been subject to suffering, but this suffering is of a very different dimension, as Paul D suffers precisely as a victim of slavery. Again like the biblical Paul, he brings redemptive news for Sethe making her realize that she is her own "best thing" (*Beloved* 273). He makes a new covenant with Sethe and in the process gets regenerated. Thus, Morrison's Paul exhibits points of conflation with, as well departure from, his biblical namesake. Driven both by desire and goodness of spirit, Paul D is a complex figure that invites mixed response. Though Wilfred D Samuels and Clenora Hudson-Weems assert that Paul D is a Christ figure (Hudson-Weems 134), one would be more near the mark by counter-arguing that Paul D, like Milkman and Son, is a character beset with ambivalent nature.

With her seventh novel *Paradise* (1998), Morrison turns her attention to a relatively obscure area of American history. *Paradise* has two overlapping stories that converge at the end. One is about the formation of the all-black town Ruby and its citizens; and the 'other' story is about a place called Convent and the five women who come to live there and through their way of living incur the wrath of the patriarchal towns-people. Written in a layered narrative, the novel is divided into nine sections, each named after a woman. The novel relates how the town Ruby came into being: the Morgan twins created it following the model of Haven, an all-black town. They named the new town after their dead sister, and following the example of Haven built a communal oven at the heart of Ruby. It also relates the story of the construction of the Convent, which was originally an embezzler's mansion, and later came to be used as a school for the Native American girls. In course of time, it gets almost deserted and becomes the shelter for runaway women. The novel covers the tales of these women as well as of a few women from the town itself. There also runs another parallel theme; a difference in the worship pattern represented by Rev. Misner and Rev. Pullium. By manipulating the themes Morrison brings out the sexism and racism inherent among the black people themselves.

In the chapter titled "Seneca" we find a controversy around the inscription on the Oven which is no longer functional, but still serves as a symbol of the community life. The younger generation demands it should be changed from "Beware the Furrow of His Brow" to "Be the Furrow of His Brow". The old-timers find this demand sacrilegious and the two priests of the town fight over it. When suggested that the inscription came from 'Big Papa' (called Zechariah), the grandfather of the Morgan twins and the founder of Haven, the young people refuse to accept it and assert "No ex-slave would tell us to be scared all the time. To 'beware' God. To be always ducking and diving, trying to look out every minute in case He's getting ready to throw something at us, keep us down" (*Paradise* 84). The town's historian Patricia thinks that the inscription could be an inscription warning outsiders, both whites and light-skinned blacks. The old-timers base their belief in Esther Morgan's 'finger memory', made from passing her fingers over letters she was too young to understand.

Esther is a conspicuous name in the *Bible*. Esther became the queen of king Xerxes and played an instrumental role not only in saving her adoptive father, Mordecai; but also in delivering her people from the scheming Haman. Turning Haman's plot on its head Esther makes Haman getting hanged at the end. The "Book of Esther" records, for later generations, the memory of a great deliverance. Like Esther in the *Bible*, who is associated with a conflict between Israel and Amalekites, Esther in *Paradise*—though she never appears in the novel in person—is connected with the rift between the two generations of Ruby. The oven was originally constructed as a reminder of the disallowing of the forefathers of Ruby. This refers to the incident when they were not allowed, due to their pitch-black skin colour, to enter Fairly, a town of lighter-skinned blacks in Oklahoma. Designed to serve a communal purpose, it came to symbolize a great 'deliverance' as well. Apart from deliverance and conflict the two Esthers are connected by the theme of emendation. Originally, the "Book of Esther" did not mention God, but in "The Greek Septuagint" a religious tone was added to it. The success of Esther in saving her people, which was initially ascribed to her beauty and intelligence, eventually came to be attributed to her piety. A similar act of emendation happens in *Paradise* when a debate ensues across two generations over the inscription on the Oven. The resultant debate regarding this addition/emendation encapsulates the power struggle between the generations of the locality. The older generation's view of the originality of the inscription can be placed in the religious tradition of patience and separation; whereas the younger generation's interpretation reflects democracy, change and empowerment. Like the biblical Esther, Esther Morgan is also associated with socio-political changes.

The debate can be traced back to Zechariah Morgan as well. Called Big Papa, he led a band of 158 deep-skinned black people to the site of Haven, an all-black town that he founded. Ruby's historian Patricia Best Cato finds out that the name Zechariah is a self-chosen one; "He renamed himself. Coffee was his birth name—a misspelling of Kofi, perhaps" (*Paradise* 192). The name Zechariah is directly lifted from the *Bible* which mentions four Zechariahs: the son of Jehoiada, stoned by the populace; the minor prophet after the exile; the father of John the Baptist to whom an angel appeared to announce the forthcoming birth to his wife Elizabeth; and the son of Baris. Patricia mentions two of them in relation to Coffee. She muses:

> Zachariahs, father of John the Baptist? or the Zechariah who had visions? the one who saw scrolls of curses and women in baskets; the one who saw Joshua's filthy clothes changed into rich ones, who saw the result of disobedience. The punishment for not showing mercy or compassion was a scattering among all nations, and pleasant land

> made desolate. All of that would fit nicely for Zechariah Morgan: the curse, the women stuffed into a basket with a lid of lead and hidden away in a house, but especially the scattering… [It] would have appealed to him if he had heard some mighty preacher tell the story of Joshua crowned. He would not name himself after Joshua, the king, but after the witness to whom God and angels spoke on a regular basis about things Coffee knew something about. (*Paradise* 192)

'Zechariah' is also the name of the penultimate book of the 'Old Testament'. It describes the harsh conditions of life in Judah after the return from exile. Zechariah followed Haggai in urging the rebuilding of the Temple, the earthly throne of the divine king. This book mentions eight visions which are linked by the theme of the consecration of Joshua as high priest. The visions decree that the land is to be cleansed of all who do not observe the Law and they promise God's continuing protection of Jerusalem. Critics have doubted the authenticity of the chapters from 9 to 14 of the book as they cite differences in styles and other compositional features.

The doubt over authorship can be connected with the debate over the inscription on the Oven which is supposed to be written by Zechariah himself. Other parallels can be drawn as well; the construction of the Temple in the *Bible* and the construction of the Oven in *Paradise* for instance. The Oven symbolized for the deep-skinned blacks, who called them '8 rocks' after the shade of black found deep in coal mines, a sense of companionship and camaraderie and represented nothing short of a religious sanctuary. Again, like his biblical namesake, Zechariah in *Paradise* is also a guide to his people. The name means 'The Lord remembers', and the story of Zechariah shows that the lord actually remembers his promises and takes care to fulfill them. His promise comes to Zechariah through a series of visions. But, whereas the biblical Zechariah guides people who are spiritually lost, Morrison's Zechariah has to guide his people who are lost empirically in the historical-cultural sense. The founding of Haven takes place after Zechariah and his people are refused entry into the town Fairly. This is read by the towns-people in divine light as they compared this disallowing with the disallowing of Joseph and Mary, the parents of Jesus. They imagine their mission to be holy and their forefathers as martyrs. Moreover, Zechariah Morgan had religious visions of a traveling man and chose Haven's site by following him who guided them to the spot. Zechariah chose his name very aptly as his life shows affinities with his biblical model though his story unfolds against a socio-cultural backdrop far removed from that of the biblical Zechariah.

Some of the girls in the Convent have names that have biblical connotations. Though these names do not actually correspond to names from the *Bible*, names like Consolata, Grace and Divine may be considered in the light of biblical concepts, e.g. 'consolation', 'grace' and 'divinity' respectively. In each case, the novel portrays a glaring dissimilarity between the assuring concepts alluded to and the actual disturbed life of the bearer of the name.

The name Consolata has close affinity with the biblical concept of consolation. In the 'New Testament' consolation is redemption brought about by the messiah. The life of Consolata, alias Connie, charts an interesting parallel. Young and homeless, she was stolen from the streets of Brazil by Mother Mary Agnes, and was taken to Oklahoma to live at Christ the King School for Native girls, locally known as the Convent. In a way, she is redeemed from a life of penury, but her new life is anything but a smooth sailing. The school closes down and she faces economic hardship again. Mother Mary dies leaving her alone. Her short affair with deacon (Deek) Morgan fails. By 1975 we find Connie nearly blind and wishing to die. However, she recovers from death wish and start telling the Convent women of Piedade, a beautiful singing woman who becomes a maternal figure of paradise embodied. It is Piedade who nestles Connie's head at the last scene of the novel. The name Piedade means 'compassion' in Portuguese. One may find a similarity between Consolata's position at the end and that of the Pieta position in which Mother Mary holds the dead body of Jesus in her lap. The two names, Piedade and Pieta, are also similar-sounding. Connie helps the Convent women in exorcising the ghost of the past.

Through Consolata Morrison presents a familiar conflict; the conflict between Eurocentric Christianity and religious practices of Africa. Connie is a believing Christian who for a long time "offered her body and her soul to God's Son and His Mother as completely as if she had taken the veil herself" (*Paradise* 225) and whose mission has been "to bring God and language to natives who were assumed to have neither;...to offer them...the privilege of knowing the one and only God and a chance, thereby, for redemption" (*Paradise* 227). This can be contextualized in the general experience of the blacks in America who find their ancestral religious practices to be have been erased by an over-riding religion. Connie's steadfast belief in the right ways of God is countered by Lone DuPress, Ruby's midwife. She reoriented Connie's faith by making her believe in magic and a more encompassing concept of God. In response to Consolata's emphasis on the need of faith, Lone says: "You need what we all need: earth, air, water. Don't separate God from His elements. He created it all. You stuck on dividing Him from His works. Don't unbalance His world" (*Paradise* 244).

Western traditions of Christianity, infested with a strong dose of Platonic philosophy, have separated God from His elements, spirituality from physicality. Lone brought out Connie's hidden gift, a power of ritualistic healing. Our last sight of Connie, with her head on the lap of Piedade, connects itself to the Pieta position and, thereby, analogizing Consolata with Jesus Christ. Similarly, the women of the Convent can evoke religious associations. Consolata's re-emergence at the end of the novel may be read as her re-demption and thereby making it possible for the reader to connect her name to the biblical concept of consolation. This also leads him to question the rationale of Ruby's men who thought they were the chosen people.

Grace, in the 'Old Testament', is an undeserved gift of God's love (Isaiah 63:7). In the 'New Testament' grace is linked to Jesus who represents in person God's graciousness towards mankind. Grace Gibson in *Paradise* is a girl from Alcorn who comes to the Convent after having lost her way, both geographically and metaphorically. She has an affair with K.D. Morgan but it ends bitterly. Free-spirited, sensual and liberated, Grace, however, has a past which is far from any favor, unmerited or otherwise, from God. Grace had been abandoned by her mother and has a father on death row. She is haunted by the image, from the Oakland riots, of a beautiful black boy spitting blood into his hands. Understanding that she has not approved of herself, she exorcises these images in Connie's loud dreaming sessions. She is also shot by the man of Ruby. Though we see her again at the end, her life is a glaring departure from the biblical concept associated with her name.

Similarly, the name Divine, of the (presumably) white girl (otherwise known as Pallas) simply means coming from (or related to) God. Pallas or Divine's life shows the irony of her name. She runs away with a high-school janitor to her artist mother. Later, she discovers him making love to her mother. Trying to escape from the memory she crashes her car and is chased by two men into a swamp. Distraught and pregnant, she arrives at the Convent at the age of sixteen where she delivers a baby boy. The ghosts of her past memories are again chased by Connie's healing sessions. After the massacre she disappears, but reappears again as we see her at her mother's with a baby carried on her chest and a sword in hand. The final vision of Divine leaves one with the hope of regeneration with rebellious potential, but the life she has lived strikes a departure again from the biblical concept associated with her name.

The title of the novel itself refers to a well-known biblical concept. Paradise or The Garden of Eden is a widely circulated concept in the *Bible* that denotes a heavenly place created by God wherein He created Adam and then Eve and gave them power to lord over all the animals. He decreed only one proscription: they must not taste the fruit of the Tree of Knowledge. Seduced by the serpent Eve flouts the decree and makes Adam comply as well. For this act of transgression they are cast out of paradise and other punitive measures are impinged upon them (Genesis 2 and 3). The word paradise has come to be associated with the Garden of Eden. Though in the 'Old Testament' the word is used in contexts other than a connection with Eden, in the 'New Testament' there is an association of 'paradise' with the realm of the blessed. A place of heavenly quality, one cannot, however, miss its exclusionary intonations. From the rules of living in there to the inhabitants, everything was according to the decree of God who only had the power to decide over issues related to the Garden of Eden/paradise.

The novel *Paradise* is also based upon a similar foundation of a town called Ruby. It was modeled upon an earlier town called Haven which was founded by Zechariah Morgan after receiving, what many thought to be, a divine guidance. He founded Haven after he, and his band of men, were refused entry by a town of light-skinned blacks. His grandsons, Deek and Steward, later founded Ruby following the ideals behind the formation of Haven. They remained very choosy regarding the inhabitants of Ruby, and disallowed new entries, thereby, causing inbreeding inside it. The community of Ruby is constructed upon patriarchal ideals and its social hierarchy on the color of skin; the blacker, the higher up on the scale. The women of the Convent, with their mixed racial identities and alternative ways of living, posed a threat to these men who were hell-bent upon preserving the sanctity of Ruby. Whereas God banished Adam and Eve when they had flouted His decree, the men of Ruby tried to slaughter these supposedly transgressing women. But Morrison introduces a new strand by showing the men having some serious lacunae and the women to be of redemptive possibilities. The title of the novel is charged with ironical significance as Morrison lays bare the fallacy of an effort to preserve the purity of a community in such an exclusionary and supremacist way.

One can trace nuanced references to the *Bible* in the naming of the cities founded in the novel. Haven, in the *Bible*, relates to the 'Fair Haven'—a port about midway on the southern coast of Crete. The biblical name Haven suggests a point of departure and not a safe haven (Acts 27:8, 12). Morrison's selection of the name is an act inversion as Haven, in *Paradise*, proved to be a comforting shelter for Zechariah Morgan and his followers. The name Ruby (given to the town that was modeled on Haven) also has its biblical parallel. In the *Bible* ruby is mentioned as a precious gem in comparison to which wisdom and knowledge are of course considered to be more valuable (Job 28:18 and Proverbs 21:15). Ruby is also mentioned in relation to virtuous women: "A wife of nobler character who can find? She is worth far more than rubies" (Proverbs: 31:10). One may infer that Morrison has deliberately played with such an association in *Paradise*. To the conventional and patriarchal men of Ruby the women of the Convent are the opposite of virtuous in the conventional sense. By bringing in these references Morrison critically puts forward the latent politics that lies underneath the construction of a pure black American community.

Morrison's penultimate novel till date, *A Mercy* (2008) can be read as a prequel to *Beloved*. In *A Mercy* also we find a slave mother who, though does not murder her children, gives her daughter away to someone who she thinks would be a better slave-master than the one she has been serving. *A Mercy* is set at a time just preceding the phase depicted in *Beloved*, before bonded labor became a principal foundation of American wealth, when that grotesque idea was just forming in the marketplace. In her collection of non-fictional essays *Playing in the Dark: The Whiteness and the Literary Imagination* (1992), Morrison contended that the history and literature of America were predicated on the exclusion of the black part of its population, and that even such a novel as *Moby Dick* which does not directly deal with a black person, is, at the bottom, marked by an anxiety regarding the black presence. She also contended that the myths of nation-building contained an explicit or an unspoken 'us' and 'them'. *A Mercy* captures the time of nation-building and is set against a backdrop of nascent America.

It captures the story of Jacob Vaark, who has come to America from Europe as a distantly related uncle leaves him 200 acres of land in the new nation and settles down to run a farm with the help of Rebekka, his young wife who comes down from England, and three black women—Lina, their native American servant whom they take in as an orphan, Sorrow, the daughter of a sea-captain and an unskilled one; and Florens, whom Vaark brings from a farm run by Senor D'Ortega to relieve Rebekka of the pain of having lost their first born Patrician. The novel also rings with references of a rebellion which was enraged in Virginia in 1675 and was led by Nathaniel Bacon. Known as the 'people's war', this rebellion is alluded to by the narrator; "Half a dozen years ago an army of blacks, natives, whites, mulattoes—freedmen, slaves and indentured—had waged war against local gentry led by the members of the very class" (*A Mercy* 8). The rebellion was thwarted but this sets the premise for the novel which unfolds against a backdrop of civil unrest, a time when persecution in the name of religion was quite common as the New England colonies labeled themselves as 'Bible Commonwealths' and tried to follow the dictates of the *Bible* in the verbatim. This was a time when slavery was still not based on skin color, and even the Europeans were also enslaved. Vaark's farm itself has two European slaves, Willard and Scully.

As is the habit of Morrison, the names she chooses for her characters are almost always imbued with significant import. Interestingly, here in *A Mercy* she ascribes the white characters with biblical names. The most prominent is Jacob Vaark himself whose first name Jacob is lifted straight from the *Bible*. Jacob, in the *Bible*, is the name of the younger son of Isaac and Rebekah. He was the favorite of his mother who helped him to deceive his father to earn his blessing instead of Esau and also usurp the rights of a first-born. To save himself from the wrath of his elder brother, Jacob flees, at his mother's suggestion, to the land of Haran. There he married Rachel and Leah and gave birth to twelve sons and a daughter with them and their maidservants Bilhah and Zilpah. He outwits his father-in-law Laban and, years later, comes back to his paternal land of Canaan where he appeases Esau, the brother he had wronged earlier. Though Jacob received the blessings of God through a vision of a ladder (known as 'Jacob's ladder'), the vision also signified that the Jewish people would be exiled and suffer before the arrival of the Messiah. A theme of exile is also implicit in Jacob Vaark's life as he comes (self-exiled) to the New World from Europe. But, unlike the biblical Jacob, he is not blessed with children as his three children died as infants and his first-born Patrician also dies at the age of five by a kick from a horse.

We may conjecture another parallel between the two. When the biblical Jacob fled to Haran, he had to look after the cattle there and presumably lived a life of hardship. If hardship can be seen as the parallel between the two namesakes, then the Jacob in *A Mercy* is pitted against a more difficult battle as he does not possess much expertise in plantation. Lina, his long-time comrade, feels both exasperated and sympathetic at this:

> More than once when Lina brought his dinner to whatever field or woodlot he was working in, she found him, head thrown back, staring at the sky as if in wondering despair at the land's refusal to obey his will. Together they minded the fowl and starter stock; planted corn and vegetables. But it was she who taught him how to dry the fish they caught; to anticipate spawning and how to protect a crop from night creatures. Yet neither of them knew what to do about fourteen days of rain or fifty-five of none. They were helpless when black flies descended in scarves, disabling cattle, the horse, and forcing them to take refuge indoors. Lina didn't know too much herself, but she did know what a poor farmer he was. (*A Mercy* 47)

Jacob Vaark's relation with his maidservant is one of camaraderie, and though she joins him in production, this production is agricultural, not biological. Morrison's Jacob portrays the hardship that the planters faced in the early days of America and through him she presents an authentic picture of that time.

In another interesting reading Jacob Vaark could be related to Noah as well. Vaark can be read as Virginia's ark. The legendary story of Noah is related to God's wrath at the people's sinful ways and the resultant deluge of forty days and nights that wiped out life of the world. God saved Noah, a holy and righteous man, and his family, and commanded him to build a huge ark to give shelter to "two of all living creatures, male and female, to keep them alive" with him (Genesis 6:19). Jacob is also interested in preserving life against a hostile environment, though in a very dissimilar context. The story reads "1682 and Virginia was still a mess" (*A Mercy* 9); and Jacob struggles through this messy environment. Like Noah, whose ark represented life in all its variations available at the time, Jacob's farm also puts forward a representative picture of the social system of that time. He got his wife (a white woman) and Lina (a black woman) through advertisements, Sorrow from a sea-captain, and Florens as a payment from a debtor. Apart from the black women who slave for him, he also enlists the help of Willard and Scully, two European slaves in addition to a blacksmith who comes from outside. Another point of parallel is that Jacob is enthused by a man called Peter Downes to cultivate rum as '[i]ts price and demand becoming greater than tobacco's now that glut was ruining the market' (*A Mercy* 27). In the *Bible* Noah is also mentioned as 'a man of the soil, [who] proceeded to plant a vineyard' (Genesis 9:20). Unlike Noah, Jacob Vaark is not blessed with children who stay alive, but like his significant namesake in shaping the history of humankind Jacob too proves instrumental in a way in shaping the history of slavery; his investment in the Barbados plantations, one of his last acts in the novel, represents the moment when it was determined that the engine of capitalism in the New World would be slave labor in distant lands.

Jacob's wife is named Rebekka. Her name is also taken from the *Bible*. Rebekah, in the *Bible,* is the mother of Jacob and Esau and the wife of Isaac. The *Bible* records how Rebekah was transported from a foreign land by a servant of Abraham to be married to Isaac (Genesis 24). Her parents give her away but we note from the beginning her decisive character, which appears in every line of the narrative, and prepares the reader to find in subsequent chapters the positive, ambitious and energetic woman that she proves herself. In *A Mercy*, Rebekka was similarly given away by her father to be married to a man in a distant land and she was transported via a ship called 'Angelus'. She is also marked by a similar strength of character that she eventually musters and runs the farm when Jacob Vaark dies. In the *Bible* Rebekah couldn't produce a child for twenty years and her namesake in *A Mercy* is similarly marked by a grief over the loss of her four children that has "unleavened her" (*A Mercy* 19). Though Rebekah was able to give birth after the initial twenty years, Rebekka remained childless after the death of her four children. She even questioned the omniscience of God at this juncture: "I don't think God knows who we are. I think He would like us, if He knew us, but I don't think He knows about us" (*A Mercy* 78). Morrison strikes a parallel between the two of the namesakes by matching their marital situation, their transportation to foreign lands, and their decisive characters. However, she also highlights a significant gap between the two as Morrison's Rebekka is pitted in an environment that is distinctly dissimilar from that of her biblical namesake and represents the basic situation of the life of a white woman in early America.

Lina's name is a shortened form of Messalina which was given by the Presbyterians; "They named her Messalina, just in case, but shortened it to Lina to signal a sliver of hope" (*A Mercy* 45). Though not exactly taken from the *Bible*, the name Messalina carries ecclesiastical resonance. It is the name of a virgin martyr and disciple of St. Felician, the Bishop of Foligno, Italy. Denounced as a Christian, she was ordered to sacrifice to the pagan gods. Her refusal resulted in her being stoned to death. Lina's life is similarly marked by a strong allegiance to her master and mistress for both of whom she becomes a comrade and helps them maintaining the farm. Though she doesn't die at the end and "continue[s] to do her work carefully", an avid observer like Scully could find that "she [is] simmering. Like green apples trembling in boiling water too long, the skin near to breaking, needing quick removal, cooling before mashed into sauce…she [is] about to burst" (*A Mercy* 143).

The title can be seen in connection with the Book; mercy in the *Bible* stands for loving-kindness, and implies the loyalty of God to the covenant. In the 'New Testament' God's mercy is revealed in the salvation offered through Jesus (Luke 1:58; Romans 11:30-2) and a similar over-glowing compassion towards human suffering is shown by Jesus (Luke 17:13). Morrison employs the word in a completely different context. It started with a mother's request to Jacob Vaark to take her daughter from the D'Ortega plantations with him as a slave. Jacob accepted the offer thinking that it would please his wife who has lost a daughter recently. However, initially it seems an inhuman act and it appeared that the mother was trying to save her own neck when she cried ""Please, Senhor. Not me. Take her. Take my daughter"" (*A Mercy* 24). This is apparently a cruel act as a mother is traditionally known to be a protector of her children and not one who gives them away. However, after an engrossing journey through a layered narrative a secret is revealed. We come to know that the giving away of the child is no inhuman act but an act of deep love as the mother sacrificed the child in the hope of giving her a better life. The voice of the mother can be heard at the end:

> One chance, I thought. There is no protection but there is difference. You stood there in those shoes and the tall man laughed and said he would take me to close the debt. I knew Senhor would not allow

> it. I said .you. Take you, my daughter. Because I saw the tall man see you as a human child, not pieces of eight. I knelt before him. Hoping for a miracle. He said yes.
>
> It was not a miracle. Bestowed by God. It was a mercy. Offered by a human. (*A Mercy* 164-65)

For a mother to give away her child without having any hope of seeing her again for what she thinks to be a better life is indeed an act of great sacrifice, and an act of mercy to understand which one must employ a different set of parameters. Stripping the word of its biblical connotation, Morrison re-situates in a human context and puts forward a telling and poignant tale of life under slavery.

The name Sorrow is an instance of a transfer of biblical concept to a name. The *Bible* records sorrow of two kind: "Godly sorrow brings repentance that leads to salvation and leaves no regret, but worldly sorrow brings death" (2 Corinthians 7:10). The latter is a sorrow of selfish kind and has nothing to with God. That is why it brings death. The former, on the other hand, finds its manifestation in repentance which results in divine grace. No such promise of a godly presence is made to Sorrow in A Mercy. In the novel Sorrow whom Jacob Vaark bought from a sea captain. No one knows about her birth and she remains a mystery as she hardly communicates with anyone and lives a solitary life in the farm. Her life, true to her name, seems to be wholly overpowered by grief. However, in an affirmation of her identity, she falls in love with the blacksmith who comes to work in the farm and is set on a search for him when Rebekka falls severely ill. Sorrow gives birth to a child (the novelist keeps the identity of the father ambiguous) and changes her name to 'Complete'. The *Bible* proposes that completion or fulfillment can only be achieved in relation to God. In *A Mercy*, however, Morrison posits a different meaning where the unmitigated sorrow of one can be mitigated by the affirmation of self-identity.

Reading these novels one can see that through these evocations Morrison invites us to consider the points of conflation between the source icon and its Afro-American adaptation; at the same time the very semblance leads us further to notice points of departure from the same source. Morrison's use of the biblical names is an act of negotiation between points of fissure and fusion and the proportionate prominence of either of the two depends on the specific context. In her use of the biblical names Morrison is not one-dimensional. Son (*Tar Baby*) elicits evocative assonance and Sethe's (*Beloved*) name remains an instance of subversion. Though wrought in different contexts, the character of Zachariah (*Paradise*) is one conspicuous example of Morrison's use of a study in parallel; and Jacob Vaark (*A Mercy*) exemplifies a synthesis of two different names to signify an instance of re-inscription.

Biblical names are use sometimes as leitmotifs by Morrison. She also uses them with the aim of critiquing the over-arching biblical frame of reference. She executes a layering of the original associations by means of varying additions, subtractions, re-inscriptions that lead to moments when meanings explode. Such an explosion gives birth to the possibilities of alternative meanings, meanings that are pertinent to the African American life. It is interesting indeed to see how Morrison's very act of calling up a hoary source-tale would make a figure or a sequence in her novel so unmistakably relevant to the context of the Black America she depicts. However, it is unmistakable to note that her us of the biblical names is marked by ambivalence: she can't go away from the 'Book' or ignore it. Yet, she can't accept it just as it has been handed down to 'them'. Hence her departures.

WORKS CITED

Barker, Kenneth L. ed. *New International Version Study Bible*. Michigan: Zondervan, 2004. (All citations from the *Bible* used in this dissertation refer to this text).

Borges, Jorge Luis. "Three Versions of Judas". *Ficciones*. 1944. New York: Grove Press, 1962. 151-58.

Canetti, Elias. *The Agony of Flies*. 1992. New York: Farrar, Strauss & Giroux, 1994.

Guth, Deborah. ""Wonder what God had in mind": *Beloved*'s Dialogue with Christianity". *Journal of Narrative Technique* 24 (1994): 83-97.

LeClair, Thomas. "The Language Must Not Sweat: A Conversation with Toni Morrison". *Conversations with Toni Morrison*. Ed. Danille Taylor-Guthrie. Jackson: UP of Mississippi, 1994. 119-28.

Morrison, Toni. *Tar Baby*. 1981. London: Vintage, 1997.

——. *Beloved*. 1987. London: Vintage, 1997.

——. *Paradise*. 1997. London: Vintage, 1999.

——. *A Mercy*. London: Chatto & Windus, 2008.

——. *Playing in the Dark: Whiteness and the Literary Imagination*. Cambridge MA: Harvard University Press, 1992.

O'Neale, Sondra. "Inhibiting Midwives, Usurping Creators: The Struggling Emergence of Black Women in American Fiction". *Feminist Studies/ Critical Studies*. Ed. Teresa DeLauretis. Bloomington: Indiana University Press, 1986. 139-56.

Otten, Terry. "The Crime of Innocence: *Tar Baby* and the Fall Myth". *Toni Morrison: Contemporary Critical Essays.* Ed. Linden Peach. New York: St. Martin's Press, 1998: 43-51. New Casebooks Ser.

Samuels, Wilfred D. and Clenora Hudson-Weems. *Toni Morrison*. Boston: Twayne Publishers, 1990.

❑❑❑

Statement about Ownership and other Particulars of

The Atlantic Critical Review

FORM IV (See Rule 8)

Place of Publication	:	New Delhi
Periodicity of the Publication	:	Quarterly
Printer's Name	:	Manish Kumar
Nationality	:	Indian
Address	:	B-2, Vishal Enclave, New Delhi 110027
Publisher's Name	:	Manish Kumar
Nationality	:	Indian
Address	:	B-2, Vishal Enclave, New Delhi 110027
Editor's Name	:	Mohit K. Ray
Nationality	:	Indian
Address	:	77, Green Park, Burdwan, West Bengal-713104
Names and addresses of individuals who own the newspaper and partners or shareholders holding more than one per cent of the total capital	:	K.R. Gupta B-2, Vishal Enclave New Delhi-110027

I, Manish Kumar, hereby declare that the particulars given above are true to the best of my knowledge and belief.

Sd/-

Date : 1st January, 2015

MANISH KUMAR
Publisher

Victim to be a Victor: Margaret Atwood's Survival Tactics in *The Edible Woman* and *Surfacing*

J.S. KIRUBAHAR AND K.S. BALAJI

MARGARET Atwood's *The Edible Woman* and *Surfacing* are written to prove that women can survive in the male-dominated world or patriarchal dominance. Marian in *The Edible Woman* bakes the cake and asks the patriarchy to eat it. The nameless protagonist of *Surfacing* challenges the patriarchy, which has erased her child in her womb, to make love and feel the child surfacing in her womb. Theirs is a challenge to the patriarchal dominance. They succeed and survive.

Atwood's feminist perspective means defining an individual selfhood without being hampered by the patriarchal myths of traditional femininity and masculinity. Women who passively accept traditional feminine roles and gain the approval and admiration of the male world are not depicted as successful. Women, who simply move to 'male' roles and seek to become individuals by oppressing other people are not considered successful. Only the nonconformist women who carve out a special place for themselves in the society without seeking power and without isolating themselves from the male world are considered successful in Atwood's novel. The women who are discussed in this chapter play leading roles in Atwood's novels and they finally transcend the gender constraints successfully. Though only a few of them observably achieve selfhood at the end, all these characters start to resist patriarchal pressure and move towards individuation near the end. Due to Atwood's realistic story-telling skills, each female character examined in this chapter is unique, and the forms of oppression and subversion differ from novel to novel. However, there are interesting parallels among them. All of them, surprisingly, start their life as traditional women who are effortlessly exploited by the patriarchal society. All of them have unhappy childhood which they reexamine in order to make sense of their sufferings in the present. All of them resort to some sort of psychological escape to create for themselves an illusion of emotional well-being. All of them live with a hidden craving to free themselves from social constraints. All of them use creative strategies to gradually invalidate the effects of their social conditioning and to achieve emotional freedom. Over all, the successful women characters discussed in this chapter are a clear exemplification of Atwood's feminist philosophy. They are the protagonists in her novels and it is through them that one listens to Atwood's authorial voice.

In *The Edible Woman*, Marian MacAlpin is portrayed as a thoughtful university graduate in her twenties, who is financially self-reliant. She lives in Toronto and shares an apartment with another young woman, Ainsley Tewce. The novel is a clear description of the phases she goes through in her rise against the social norms prescribed by the male-dominated society. Satirically, Marian, out of necessity, has to live in an old building with a nosy and meddlesome lady in the ground floor and the restrictive nature of the building, parallels that of the society itself. In the beginning, she chooses to live according to the norms of the society with a complete awareness of the expectations of the male-dominated society and the acceptable norms of gender relations. However, through her relationships with different types of characters in the novel, she comes to know how women are subjugated and "she becomes increasingly disillusioned with her job and her fiancé, Peter Wollander, to the point where her inner conflict finds its outward expression in an eating disorder whose symptoms resemble anorexia nervosa" (Howells 2005: 24).

In part 1 of the novel, all characters and situations are viewed through Marian's eyes, and therefore the narration is in the first person. Atwood seems to use this narrative strategy to indicate the subjective and the limited nature of the perspective. It is her company, Seymour Surveys, which gives Marian an initial (but a crucial) understanding of how women are being marginalized and forced to accept certain 'socially acceptable' roles. Seymour Surveys is "layered like an ice cream sandwich, with three floors" (13). The top floor is occupied only by men who have responsible and respectable positions. In other words, it is the 'decision-making floor'. The bottom, on the other hand, is full of machines/operatives. The middle layer which Marian belongs to is the link between the two. "Marian soon realizes that she is literally and figuratively trapped" (Tandon 2009: 37). She feels great anxiety and uncertainty about her role in the company.

> What then could I expect to turn into at Seymour Surveys? I couldn't become one of the men upstairs; I couldn't become a machine person or one of the questionnaire-marking ladies, as that would be a step down. (14)

Seymour Surveys also has certain practices that discriminate against women. The Manager, Mrs. Bogue thinks women who get pregnant are disloyal to the company: "I'm afraid Mrs. Dodge in Kamloops will have to be removed. She's pregnant" (21). Moreover, her job as a market researcher enables her to realize how humiliating it is for a woman to do something which is not conventionally appropriate for women. The extract below shows Marian's experience with a man she meets during a survey on men's beer consumption.

> …I saw him lurching out of his chair towards me with a beery leer. 'Now what's a nice little girl like you doing walking around asking men all about their beer?' he said moistly. 'You ought to be at home with some big strong man to take care of you.' (52)

She finds the attitude adopted by Seymour Surveys and the public extremely vexing, but as a meek social conformist, she often, till the end of the second part of the novel, behaves in a passive manner and creates an impression that she is a supporter of male dominion. McWilliams (2006) says, "In her (Marian) work as a market researcher […] she is accomplice to, as well as victim of, the mass consumerism that she later identifies as defining her relationship with her fiancé, Peter." (67)

Marian spends weekends with Peter Wollander, a young lawyer who has an ardent fascination for guns and cameras. Their relationship has a highly symbolic value in the novel as Marian represents Canadian passivity, while Peter is a typical symbol of American consumerism and imperialism. Their first sexual experience only frustrates Marian as Peter's attention is directed more towards cleaning off the pieces of glass that gets broken. On another occasion, Peter takes Marian into the bathroom because he wants love under shower. Marian thinks this is perhaps Peter's "attempt to assert youthfulness and spontaneity" (68). Peter does not care about how inconvenient it is for her, but Marian, in spite of her physical discomfort, remains submissive and tries to satisfy him: "…I knew the tub would be too small and uncomfortably hard and ridged, but I hadn't objected" (68).

It is very clear that Atwood uses sex in *The Edible Woman* "to evoke masculine blindness to the women's point of view" (Inamdar 2002:

183). It also exposes women's passivity and how it facilitates their own victimization. Marian, being a subservient young woman, willingly loses her personality, and in Peter's presence, she only reflects Peter's image of herself: "As we stared at each other in that brief light I (Marian) could see myself, small and oval, mirrored in his (Peter's) eyes" (98). In other words, Marian willingly accepts the restrictive gender roles imposed upon women in paternalist society. Regarding Marian's passivity, Salat (1994) says:

> If Peter's—the male's—imperialistic designs are condemnable, Marian's—the female's self-willed subservience is no less blame-free. In Atwood's exposition of gender-politics, therefore, woman is as much implicated in the processes that perpetuate male hegemony as is man. (97)

However, Marian seems only to accept the social destiny of women in the patriarchal system. Women's biological destiny which is celebrated by her friends, Ainsley and Clara, on the other hand, only evokes a feeling of aversion in her. Atwood comically dramatizes the ambiguities and inconsistencies within the notion of 'femininity' by juxtaposing the subservient Marian with "two parodic versions of earth-mothers" (Howells 2005: 23): Clara, who is a passive victim of women's biological destiny and Ainsley, who hatches a cunning plot to find a father for her child. Neither of them is acceptable to Marian, and this shows that she is going through an identity crisis. Pourgharib (2008) rightly says she "represents the younger generation of women, which considers itself drifting along without any sense of direction" (87).

Marian agrees to Peter's proposal of marriage as she thinks it is unavoidable and can make her life better by providing some sort of stability. She thinks Peter is attractive and bound to be successful: ""'When do you want to get married?' he asked almost gruffly.... I'd rather have you decide that. I'd rather leave the big decisions up to you" (107). Marian's reply shows more of her belief that she is required to depend on Peter (or any other man for that matter) than any personal exhilaration. She also seems to think that she as a woman cannot make major decisions. That Marian's entire personality is a social construct is made evident in Pourgharib's remark:

> The kind of pressure that drives her towards the marriage institution is by no means coercive or imposed from above: the pressure is rather psychological, ideological and cultural which have structured

> her subjectivity and ego that constantly bar her from thinking or doing anything that is socially branded as 'abnormal' or 'perverse'. (2008: 90)

Though Peter uses her for his own benefit, she persuades herself that she has to comply with his wishes. With reference to the victim positions postulated by Atwood in *Survival,* Tandon (2009) contends that "at the beginning of the novel, Marian occupies victim position number two-acknowledgment of the fact of being a victim but the acceptance of it as something inevitable" (42). Her acceptance of her own victimization should not be viewed as an individual choice, but as a sign of how malevolent patriarchal values have been strongly and craftily established in the society.

In spite of the insidious effects of the discriminating social system she lives in, Marian, out of her experiences with various characters in the novel and her own perceptiveness, becomes disillusioned with Peter and marriage. She soon becomes acutely conscious of how Peter is using her for his own benefit. She realizes that he shows no consideration for her feelings and that he takes her everlasting presence and submissiveness for granted. There is a shift from first person to third person narration in Part 2 befitting Marian's loss of an independent sense of self. Interestingly, Clara seems to be one of the initial catalysts that trigger off a change in Marian's attitude towards matrimony and motherhood. Marian has always found sexually mature female bodies rather sickening. She likens Clara's pregnant body to "a boa-constrictor that has swallowed a watermelon" (30). It "seemed somehow beyond her (Clara), going its own way without reference to any directions of hers" (37). The way Marian disapprovingly views Clara's wretched life with her children in the beginning of the novel shows that there is an innate aversion in her to the traditional roles imposed on women, which is often eclipsed by her outward social conformity. Perhaps, it is this conflict in her that later urges her to set out to free herself from the social restrictions and discover her selfhood. Later in the novel, she visits Clara in a maternity hospital and when she leaves the hospital, she feels greatly relieved: "She had the sense of having escaped, as if from a culvert or cave. She was glad she wasn't Clara" (161).

According to Pourgharib (2008), "Clara provides Marian a foresight of what she will end up becoming if she gets married to Peter" (90). The fear of losing her identity and freedom to Peter, therefore, grows in her as marriage nears. She begins to doubt if she has made a right decision. Her consciousness of her own victimization in Peter's manipulative hands becomes painfully intense when she watches Peter eating:

> Watching him operating on the steak like that, carving a straight slice and then dividing it into neat cubes, made her think of the diagram of the planned cow at the front of one of her cookbooks; the cow with lines on it and labels to show you from which part of the cow all the different cuts were taken.... She could see rows of butchers somewhere in a large room, a butcher school, sitting at tables...cutting out steaks.... (185)

She thinks that she herself has become an object of consumption, devoured by Peter with great delight. The fear of being consumed makes her extremely repugnant to meat and she cannot eat meat anymore: "She looked down at her own half-eaten steak and suddenly saw it as a hunk of muscle. Blood Red. Part of a real cow that once moved and ate and was killed..." (185).

The more unreliable her relationship with Peter, the more distressed she becomes and her anxiety results in a growing antipathy towards food and she hates to eat anything. As Peter gains more power over her, she hysterically starts identifying herself with the hunted and consumed. "As her marriage gets closer, so her disorder gets worse and the list of 'forbidden foods' gets longer, until the point where she can eat nothing at all" (Howells 2005: 29). Her anxiety about the possibility of losing her independent social identity through marriage to Peter results in an overt physical disorder—complete loss of appetite. It looks as though Marian suffers from anorexia nervosa, but Howells (2005) argues that "it is a pathological condition of self-division—a division of head and body at the neck" (27).

Simone de Beauvoir says that woman's body offers a tough resistance to the unfair demands that the society and nature make on it. In other words, even though Marian is willing to give into the demands of the patriarchal social system, her body revolts against them. "It is Marian's very metabolism that is most rebellious to her efforts at metamorphosing into a social-cultural conformist" (Pourgharib 2008: 89). This is because Marian has intrinsically rejected the models of adult women represented by Clara, Ainsley and the office virgins, and her fear of growing into any of the model that conforms to the social standards stops her from giving any further sustenance to her body. Though Marian is terrified by this problem and thinks that she "will starve to death," (186), from the perspective of her search for selfhood, her eating disorder needs to be interpreted as a major step forward. Marian's eating disorder marks a positive moment of change and transformation and it represents a political act of resistance. Her rejection of food is caused by her subconscious rejection of the victim role and this means she is now in victim position number three: acknowledgement of the fact of being consumed and assimilated by Peter (Tandon 2009: 42).

However, to Marian, her eating disorder is just a baffling illness until Duncan makes her understand its significance by relating it to an inner rebellion by saying, "You're probably representative of modern youth, rebelling against the system" (236). Marian meets Duncan when she was doing a survey for Moose Beer. She meets him again at the Laundromat and is instinctively attracted by him. It is fitting that her relationship with Duncan, who is weak and puny, becomes stronger as her eating disorder gets worse. What she really likes about Duncan is that he, unlike Peter, does not have any expectations that she has to meet.

> …when he (Duncan) would murmur…. 'You know, I don't even really like you very much,' it didn't disturb her at all because she didn't have to answer. But when Peter…would whisper 'I love you' and wait for the echo, she had to exert herself. (227)

This frank and unpretentious nature of Duncan is a crucial element in Marian's journey to self-discovery. Since there is no pressure on her to conform, she can be herself, Marian. Thus, she, in the company of Duncan, gets an opportunity to self-examine and reassess herself in relation to others and slowly acquire a new awareness of herself. Now, she can perceive more clearly the covert dominion that Peter has over her and she is filled with a sense of impending doom. What annoys her more is "his maneuvers to squeeze Marian into a model identity based on his own propensities and prejudices as to how a woman should be" (Pourgharib 2008: 97).

While she is in the bath just before her engagement party, she begins to feel that "she was dissolving, coming apart layer by layer like a piece of cardboard in a gutter puddle" (274). She feels very uneasy because she thinks that Peter has manipulated her cleverly, made her do things she never liked and nearly erased her true personality. Once she gets dressed up and (heavily) made up for the event, Peter is pleased and says "Darling, you look absolutely marvelous" (287), but this compliment only saddens her as she feels Peter has succeeded in tearing her away from her true self. She thinks what she sees reflected in the mirror is not herself but a fake:

> Her attention caught on the various details, the things she wasn't used to—the fingernails, the heavy earrings, the hair, the various parts of her face.... What was it that lay beneath the surface these pieces were floating on, holding them all together? (287)

Nonetheless, she is still a "socio-cultural" conformist trying to perform her role to the satisfaction of Peter and other guests. She puts on a welcoming countenance in the engagement party while her inner self feels completely alienated. She entertains the guests smilingly but her mind is filled with a sense of detachment. Though part 2 is in the third person narration, Atwood's use of phrases like '*soap-men*' and '*soap-wives*' (303) to refer to the guests, skillfully indicate Marian's cynical view of the social system and the falsity of the so-called socially appropriate gender roles and behavior. Kindled by the extreme inner-conflict, she starts simmering with frustration. Her sense of victimization is further fueled by Joe's comments on the effects of marriage on women:

> When she gets married, her core gets invaded.... Her core. The centre of her personality, the thing she's built up; her image of herself.... Her feminine role and her core are really in opposition, her feminine role demands passivity from her.... (296)

In that potentially explosive situation, Peter tries to take her photograph. This terrifies her because she sees Peter's camera as a symbol of the restrictive forces of the society. She thinks the photograph will trap her permanently and she will not be able to move or change. Panic-stricken, she flees like a hunted animal and retreats to Duncan with a view to saving herself. Fleeing from the party is a metaphorically significant step in Marian's quest for selfhood. All major characters that represent various alternatives available to Marian come together at Peter's party. By running away, Marian metaphorically rejects all these alternatives.

Duncan, to Marian's disappointment, proves to be deceitful and sexually exploits her. However, Atwood uses Duncan's character in such a way that his deceitfulness has a didactic value in the novel. He makes Marian understand how she has always been compliant and passive, and allowed both men in her life to use and consume her quite easily, thus helping the process of victimization. She is not angry with him as he, unlike

Peter, is very explicit about what he wants from her. Most importantly, he makes her shed all those carefully nurtured pretences and turn into her true self: "I'm not letting you into this bed until you go in there and peel that junk off your face" (319).

Prompted by Duncan to go back and fight her way through her predicament individually, she returns to her place and bakes a cake in the shape of a woman which is intended to be her own image. The process of making the 'cake woman' makes her ruminate on the wretched destiny of a woman in the society. Staring at the cake, she realizes her own complicity in her victimization, and she tells herself, "You look delicious.... Very appetizing. And that's what will happen to you; that's what you get for being food" (342). When Peter comes to see her, she offers the cake to him and says, "You've been trying to destroy me, haven't you.... You've been trying to assimilate me. But I've made you a substitute, something you'll like much better..." (344). Peter is alarmed and immediately leaves the place. Choosing cake-making, a traditionally feminine act, to express her resistance clearly shows she is not willing to shed her femininity but only her willingness to be consumed by the patriarchal social system.

Once Peter leaves, Marian is relieved that her womanhood, which she would have lost to Peter, is safe. Consequently, her body returns to normal metabolism. She feels very hungry and eats the cake herself. Seeing this act, her friend Ainsley exclaims in horror: "You're rejecting your femininity" (345). However, Marian's eating of the cake, by showing her control over herself, only asserts her femininity. The act of eating the cake also signifies the realignment of her body with her head. With no inner conflict, she rejoins the society. She tells Duncan over the telephone: "I realized Peter was trying to destroy me. So now I'm looking for another job" (350). This shows she is ready for renewal and reformation. Her desire is to be "a woman with an absolute, as against a relatively defined, identity" (Salat 1994: 95-96). In other words, she wants to remain a woman "not by consenting to be a part of the social mainstream, but by revolting against it" (Pourgharib 2008: 92). This renewed form of Marian clearly matches up with Atwood's creative non-victim position.

The namelessness of the protagonist of *Surfacing* helps the character effectively epitomize the social alienation that is commonly felt by people who are unable to play the roles imposed upon them by the domineering patriarchal society. She says, "I no longer have a name. I tried all those years to be civilized but I'm not and I'm through pretending" (173). The social alienation also makes her emotionally numb. She says, "I realized I did not feel much of anything, I hadn't for a long time. Perhaps I'd been like that all my life, just as some babies are born deaf or without a sense of touch" (106). She gets upset about her inability to feel and is occasionally jealous of Anna and Joe who are emotionally sound. However, from this deficient position, the protagonist "finds a way to heal the split within her own psyche, thereby restoring her emotional and spiritual health" (Howells 2005: 41) and revolts "against the denial of woman's professional aspirations as well as motherhood" (Prabhakar, M. 1999: 100).

After living in Toronto for several years, she goes back to the Quebec wilderness, the place of her childhood, to look for her lost father. However, she slowly realizes that what she is looking for in the wilderness is not her father but her own past, which holds clues to the root causes of her present problems. Her return to her childhood environment evokes memories of incidents that shaped her gender identity and of how she gradually gave in to the demands of the patriarchal system. The novel is about the narrator's psychological journey into her past only to emerge as a liberated woman. She believes that it is only by understanding and reversing the effects of her own past that she can attain selfhood. Her urge to reverse the effects of the society on her psyche to attain emotional and social purification is evident when she finally says, "Everything from history must be eliminated" (181). A study of the narrator's past will therefore reveal how the domineering, male-dominated society subdues a woman and shapes her gender identity.

First of all, her childhood memories are replete with forceful personalities of father images and dim elusive mother figures. As a child, the narrator adores her father. She is socially conditioned to identify herself with him, rather than with her insipid mother. She grows up in a male-dominated school system where it is worse for a girl to ask questions than for a boy. The boys in the school chase and capture the girls after the school and tie them up with their own skipping ropes, "silently underscoring how feminine playthings may themselves trap young girls into sexual stereotypes, thereby constraining their free development" (Gottlieb 1978: 311). Sadly, the boys tease the narrator much more vehemently as she is more reclusive and timid than other girls. "Being socially retarded is like being mentally retarded, it arouses in others disgust and pity and the desire to torment and reform" (69). Her aversion to fabricated social customs is manifest in her remarks about birthday parties:

> I despised them, the pew-purple velvet dresses with antimacassar lace collars and the presents, voices going Oooo with envy when they were opened, and the pointless games, finding a thimble or memorizing clutter on a tray. (68)

However, such 'personal opinions' are unbecoming of a girl, and the narrator is forced by her mother to conform to the social expectations and be *civilized* (69). In addition to what happens to her at school and home, her observation of what happens to other local women also seems to mould her gender consciousness. The local priest bans women from wearing short skirts and bare arms and, sincerely obeying this religious rule, many women refrain from swimming because they do not want to wear swimsuit and expose their legs and arms. Interestingly, the various developmental stages of the narrator's gender identity, due to the impact of the society, can be seen in the pictures drawn by her as a child in her scrapbooks. Her earliest scrapbook is full of semi-divine pictures, implying that she is in a state of wholeness. One of her later scrapbooks, however, has pictures of Easter eggs and rabbits. "Page after page of eggs and rabbits, grass and trees, normal and green, surrounding them, flowers blooming, sun in the upper right hand corner of each picture, moon symmetrically in the left. All the rabbits were smiling and some were laughing hilariously; several were shown eating ice-cream cones from the safety of their egg-tops" (91). This is possibly the girl's visualization of heaven. This stage represents a clear distinction between the good and the bad and a tendency to identify only with the good. The social values are beginning to impinge on the narrator's attitude. The third developmental stage is marked by a scrapbook which is full of "illustrations cut from magazines and pasted in. They were ladies, all kinds: holding up cans of cleanser, knitting, smiling, modeling toeless high heels and nylons with dark seams and pillbox hats and veils" (91). This shows that the narrator has imbibed socially determined gender principles and the meaningless fabrications created by her consumer-oriented society. It indicates that she is now a 'woman' in the patriarchal sense, ready to be controlled and exploited.

It is little wonder that her femininity and professional aspirations are easily shattered by her devious art teacher. The art teacher prevents her from developing into a real artist by discouraging her by saying that studying art will not be useful to her as "there has never been any important women artists" (49). She therefore becomes an illustrator of children's books, and also does designs and fabric patterns, a profession which does not satisfy her artistic sensibilities. She then falls prey to his seduction techniques and starts thinking of him as her husband and loves him sincerely: "I worshiped him, non-child-bride, idolater; I kept the scraps of his handwriting like saints' relics" (150). However, his relationship with the narrator is driven by pure lust. And the narrator is sexually exploited. What happens subsequently is something that leaves a deep scar in the narrator's mind and makes her emotionally numb for many years to come. When she is pregnant, her art teacher skillfully convinces her to abort the child, an immoral act that the narrator feels guilty about almost eternally: "Whatever it is, part of myself or a separate creature, I killed it. It wasn't a child but it could have been one, I didn't allow it" (144). The abortion rather effectively illustrates "the side effect of a patriarchal rational and oppressing world" (Tandon 2009: 73). The exploitation by the man she loved and the thoughts of her aborted child fill her mind with a sense of remorse and she becomes a sort of psychological suicide. Since she cannot face her own sinful past, she, like many of Atwood's protagonists, escapes into a fabricated past; she tells everyone that she is a divorcee and her child lives with her husband. However, her experience with the art teacher is a very crucial factor that changes her attitude towards men and marriage. This probably can be considered the beginning of her journey to selfhood. Her awakening is further strengthened by her visit to the place of her childhood and her observation of how Anna is ill-treated by her husband David. "She discovers that marriage is no more than a surrendering of values and distortion of the identity of a woman" (Prabhakar, M. 1999: 104). Besides, she no longer believes in love and in fact she is completely incapable of love, a defect that often maddens her boy friend, Joe.

Nevertheless, she remains an untruthful person who keeps refusing to accept her own past and draws comfort from the network of deceptions and lies that she has created. In fact, what makes her bizarre is that she herself believes in her own falsehood. All her faults, however, are expelled from her when she dives down into the lake to search for the Indian rock paintings that were recorded in her father's paintings. While swimming underwater, she sees a strange, unclear image which, she thinks, is her father's drowned body. That image brings back in her mind the painful memories that she has repressed so far and she gets the mental courage to come to terms with her real past. She confesses her falsehood finally: "I couldn't accept it, that mutilation, ruin I'd made, I needed a different version" (144). As Howells (2005: 46) points out, diving into the lake works both as a realistic description and as a metaphor for descent into the territory of the subconscious. The changes that happen to the narrator can therefore be interpreted as a pure psychological transformation, which, surprisingly, helps her recover her emotional well-being: "Feeling was beginning to seep back into me. I tingled like a foot that's been asleep" (147). She is a whole being now. Like Marian in *The Edible Woman*, who regains the ability to eat, she regains the ability to feel.

As a reformed woman, her first discernible act against the malevolent patriarchal aspirations is the destruction of the film made by David and Joe. By flinging the film reels into the water, she thinks she has released all the enslaved elements that have been captured by David and Joe, including the nudity of Anna. Her next objective is to attain motherhood which has been denied to her. This is necessary not only to respond to her new feminist consciousness but also to flush out the death that she thinks she is filled with. She believes she can bring back her aborted child alive by becoming a mother again. "Nothing has died, everything is alive, everything is waiting to become alive" (160). What is significant at this stage is that the narrator has become a conscious decision-maker, and chooses Joe, her boy friend, and takes him to the wilderness to make love. The copulation in the wilderness indicates "a symbolic rejection of the civilization and its institutions" (Ramana, P.S. 2006: 16). She feels extremely happy because she thinks she has got her child back: "He (Joe) trembles and then I can feel my lost child surfacing within me, forgiving me, rising from the lake where it has been prisoned for so long" (165). It should also be noted that a powerless woman who was used by her art teacher is now using a man, Joe, to fulfill her ambition. This clearly indicates a transfer from victim position to victor position.

However, the realization of her true self makes her sense of alienation more intense. She thinks she is totally incompatible with the 'civilized' world which wants everyone to conform to patriarchal expectations. Therefore, she discards her "human skin" that is the clothes and runs through the woods, rejecting the world that has victimized her. She starts to live like an unblemished animal that peacefully coexists with nature.

Later, "her body boundaries dissolve and she has a vision of becoming vitally connected to the earth as a component of the wilderness landscape" (Howells 2005: 47).

> 'I lean against a tree, I am a tree leaning.... I am not an animal or a tree, I am the thing in which the trees and animals move and grow, I am a place. (187)

However, her momentary separation from the civilization and the human social order gives her a greater understanding of her place in the society and an awareness that she cannot survive without society. "At the sight of a fish jumping on the lake, the narrator undergoes a series of radical shifts in perception till her vision settles back into a frame of normalcy" (Howells 2005: 47).

> From the lake a fish jumps.
> An idea of a fish jumps.
> A fish jumps, carved wooden fish with dots painted on the sides, no, antlered fish thing drawn in red on cliffstone, protecting spirit. It hangs in the air suspended, flesh turned to icon, he has changed again, returned to the water. How many shapes can he take.
> I watch it for an hour or so; then it drops and softens, the circles widen, it becomes an ordinary fish again. (193)

From this sight, the narrator clearly understands that though her immersion into her subconscious mind (symbolized by water) is very useful, she must return to the conscious level and lead a responsible life in the society. She also realizes that it is very important for her to live in order to allow her child to be born. "If I die it dies, if I starve it starves with me.... It must be born, allowed" (198). This can also be interpreted as the narrator's realization that mankind cannot survive without women. She decides to return to the society, but this time as a liberated woman who knows her place in the society: "This above all, to refuse to be a victim" (197).

WORKS CITED

Atwood, Margaret. *Survival: A thematic guide to Canadian literature.* Ontario: House of Anansi Press Limited, 1972.

——. *Surfacing.* New York: Anchor Books, 1972.

——. *The Edible Woman.* London: Virago, 1976.

Gottlieb, Lois C. and Wendy Keitner. "Colonialism as Metaphor and Experience in 'The Grass is Singing' and 'Surfacing,' Narasimhaiah (Ed.) *Awakened*

Conscience: Studies in Commonwealth Literature. New Delhi: Sterling Publishers, (1978): 307-14.

Howells, Coral Ann, *Margaret Atwood,* Second edition. New York: Palgrave Macmillan, 2005.

Inamdar, F.A. "The Feminine Predicament in Margaret Atwood's *The Edible Woman*". In Bhatnagar, Manmohan K. *Feminist English Literature*. New Delhi: Atlantic Publishers and Distributors, 2002.

McWilliams, Ellen."Margaret Atwood's Canadian Hunger Artist: Postcolonial Appetites in *The Edible Woman*." *Kunapipi* 28.2, 2006.

Pourgharib, Behzad. "Postmodernist Feminism and Margaret Atwood's *The Edible Woman*." *The Atlantic Literary Review Quarterly* 9.4 (Oct-Dec 2008).

Prabhakar, M. *Feminism/Postmodernism: Margaret Atwood's Fiction*. New Delhi: Creative Books, 1999.

Ramana, P.S. "Margaret Atwood's *Surfacing*: Critique of Novel, Matrimony and Subjectivity as Cultural Constructions." *The Literary Criterion* 41.1 (2006): 5-27.

Salat, M.F. "A Delicious Fare: Margaret Atwood's *The Edible Woman*." *Perspectives on Canadian Fiction*. Sudhakar Pandey (Ed.). New Delhi: Prestige Books, 1994: 94-105.

Tandon, Neeru and Anshul Chandra. *Margaret Atwood. A jewel in Canadian Writing*. New Delhi: Atlantic Publishers & Distributors (P) Ltd., 2009.

❑❑❑

Power Relations Dynamics in the Academe: A Close Reading of Srividya Natarajan's *No Onions Nor Garlic*

AVERI MUKHOPADHYAY AND RASHMI GAUR

"A novel, usually comic or satirical, in which the action is set within the enclosed world" of the academe "(university or similar set of learning) and highlights the follies of academic life", is termed as 'campus novel' in Chris Baldick's *The Concise Oxford Dictionary of Literary Terms* (33). Campus novel as a literary genre is relatively new. Writings on universities and life within campuses have existed but only as references in nineteenth century England in the works of Bulwer-Lytton, Benjamin Disraeli, William Thackeray, Charles Reade, Anthony Trollope, George Eliot, Samuel Butler and Thomas Hardy. Campus novels in the sense they are defined above in *The Concise Oxford Dictionary of Literary Terms*, originated in America with Mary McCarthy's *The Groves of Academe* published in 1952.

There was a surge in the production of campus novels as higher education in America and Britain increased rapidly after the Second World War drew to its close in 1945. Universities and colleges opened on a large scale and the primary objective of these newly established educational institutes in both the countries was to take in the returning war veterans. Later on the admission of a large percentage of the baby booming population in these universities accentuated their existence and significance. Gradually, these white tile and red brick universities, as they were popularly known, evolved as *in loco parentis* for students, creating a complete society on the campus, with education, housing, meals, medical care, and social life all being provided communally and institutionally. Close relations were in turn forged in such campuses among a wide range of key characters-students and faculty, parents and administrator, lecturer and professor, male and female, Black and White, low caste and high caste. This gave rise to an insider's as well as an outsider's rendering, particularly in campus novels, on the multi-dimensional relations, all of which due to the play of power eventually culminated into 'power relations'—a term used by Michel Foucault while he revisited and reconceptualised the concept 'power'. College and university campuses are indeed one of the world's most socially heterogeneous societies and here power is pervasive across caste, class, race, gender, region, religion. Power relations, as such, offer a broad scope of study and of late the book market too, especially in India is being flooded by newly published campus novels in English. Hence, in this paper, a limited range of power relations dynamics, that between professor and student, man and woman, and high caste and low caste will be considered. It is the play of power and the ways the above mentioned 'power relations' are negotiated on Foucauldian lines by individuals in a location as specific as the academe and in the context of an Indian campus novel—*No Onions Nor Garlic*, that the paper seeks to investigate and discuss.

No Onions Nor Garlic, the maiden campus novel by Srividya Natarajan, a teacher of English at King's University College, University of Western Ontario, is wildly funny almost evoking the romantic confusions in P.G. Wodehouse's Blandings Castle stories. The humour of *No Onions Nor Garlic* arouses laughter in the readers till the very end but humour works best only when it has an underlying theme: when it offers social commentary, holds power to account or simply relies on good natured storytelling to make a point. *No Onions Nor Garlic* with its backdrop of Chennai University, telling the story of an onion- and garlic-free Tamilian Brahmin who rewrites William Shakespeare's *A Midsummer Night's Dream* to uphold the Hindu order, smug NRIs who call the shots in matrimonial, visiting Canadians who are aghast at the plight of dalits (pronounced 'daylights') and, at the apex of the whole tumbling structure, a bibulous builder who invokes the gods even as he defrauds his clients is an example of humour at its best. The novel's haunting and serious issues of caste system, corruption in the academic circle, the unscrupulous builder-bureaucracy nexus convey that behind the hilarity, all is not well on and off the university campus.

There was a time, precisely before the beginning of the new millennium, when campus novels whether in India or in the western world, while being satiric and ironic were simultaneously idyllic, cosmic and mythic. Nevertheless, since October 2000, as the cultural critic Sarah Boxer had observed in an essay in the *New York Times*, the campus novel seemed suddenly bleaker (qtd. in Showalter 100). The darkly apocalyptic tone of the fiction of the new century in India had already been set in the 1990s with the publication of Makarand Paranjape's *The Narrator* but, as this form of literary genre gained prominence after 2004 with the bestselling author Chetan Bhagat, the tone became more visible and a question of concern. Hence, in *No Onions Nor Garlic*, published in the year 2006, too, tailing the ludicrous incidents is the exposure of a structurally unsound ivory tower of the academe resulting from the constant agitation against the Reservation Policy and the politicking by the upper caste Hindus to maintain a stronghold inside the premises of the university vis-à-vis the society at large. The novel spills out the challenges to the university's power structures from groups such as the lower castes, especially the dalits, the students, and women in general. While the use of power by the authority is clearly discernible in the novel, what is most hidden in it is the set of relations of power between lecturers and students, upper caste Hindus and lower caste Hindus, and men and women.

Power has always been a major area of contention since recorded history. 'Power' as a concept has fascinated philosophers, political theorists, historians and critics from Plato and Aristotle in the 4th and 3rd centuries BC respectively, to Machiavelli during the European Renaissance in the 15th century, Thomas Hobbes in the 16th century, Voltaire in the 17th century, Karl Marx, Friedrich Engels, Vladimir Lenin, and Friedrich Nietzsche in the 19th century, and Michel Foucault in the 20th century. As such, each century has witnessed the concept 'power' being redefined and undergoing significant changes. Power as a concept has always been in a state of constant flux. Plato, in his book *Republic*, written around 380 BC, mentions that the supreme ruler is a philosopher king who tries to achieve the highest level of knowledge and not one who craves for power. Plato despises any form of governance which reflects the misuse of power, as in the case of democracy where the power is wielded by the people. Aristotle's *Politics*, written sometime around 350 BC, and a rejoinder to Plato's *Republic*, contains his keen sense of the dangers of power abuse. According to Aristotle, human beings are all political animals and giving power to people may prove vituperative. Around the same period, authors from as far as China and India had also expounded, explained, and elaborated the concept of 'power'. Sun Tzu's Chinese military treatise, *The Art of War* (500 BC), Vidura's *Vidura-Niti*, and

Chanakya's *Chanakya Niti Shastra* in India are some of the significant works on power.

The concept 'power' continued to interest thinkers many centuries after the above mentioned works of ancient philosophers and statesmen were produced. This is clear from Niccolo Machiavelli's *The Prince* published in 1532, which is considered to be the seminal text of the Renaissance period in Europe. *The Prince* is a dissertation of power which lays down the famous axiom: in the arena of power the end justifies the means. Thomas Hobbes' *Leviathan* (1660) coming more than a century later also, sounds a note of caution when he says that human beings are caught in a lifelong, perpetual and restless desire for power. After all, 'power' as described in *Leviathan* is a man's "present means, to obtain some future apparent good" (Hobbes n. pag.). Voltaire, the French Enlightenment writer, also critiqued the misuse of power, especially that by the Catholic Church. The legacy of conceptualising power as the capacity of powerful agents to realise their will over the will of the powerless people, and the ability to force them to do things which they do not wish to do continued even in the political theorists and revolutionaries of the 19th century and the early 20th century like Karl Marx, Friedrich Engels and Vladimir Lenin. As a result, the Marxist school of thought despite being a 20th century phenomenon views power as a possession, something which is held onto by those who are in power and which those who are powerless try to wrest from their control. In fact, for all the political scientists discussed above including those of the Marxist School, power is seen as repression of the powerless by the powerful and it is from this 'repressive hypothesis' as Foucault himself terms, that he marks a remarkable departure. For him, power is productive. It gives birth to resistance. Countering 'power with power' creates a proper kind of resistance whereby the 'power' and 'resistance' gets blurred and the resisting agents start exercising 'power'. This benefits both the individuals involved in the power relation.

This idea of Foucault germinates in his works such as *The Birth of the Clinic* (1973), *Discipline and Punish* (1977), *The History of Sexuality* (1978) and *Power / Knowledge* (1980). In all these works, Foucault tries to shift thinking about power beyond the view of power as suppression of the powerless by the powerful to a scrutiny of the way that power operates within everyday relations between institutions and people. For it is in the relationship between the institution and the individual that we find power working most vividly. However, instead of viewing power simply in a negative way, as restraining and repressing, Foucault argues, particularly in *The History of Sexuality,* Vol. I (1978), that even at their most restricting, oppressive measures are in fact fruitful, generating new forms of behaviour rather than simply redacting certain forms of behaviour. In the same book, Foucault mentions that power is something which is performed, something which is more like a strategy rather than a possession. Interestingly, power develops into strategy due to the functioning of discourse.

Discourse, as defined by Foucault in *The Archaeology of Knowledge* is, "the general domain of all statements, sometimes as an individualizable group of statements, and sometimes as a regulated practice that accounts for a number of statements" (80). Discourse as 'the general domain of all statements' or as 'individualizable groups of statements' is viewed as a system which structures the way we perceive reality. After all, discourse as referred in the essay, "The order of discourse", is the 'violence which we do to things' (Foucault 67). This is largely because a complex set of practices manage the existence of discourses. Discourse is not just a simple set of statements which have some coherence, rather, people in positions of authority sanction certain practises which try to keep some chosen group of statements in circulation. Similarly, there are other practices also which try to ward off conflicting statements out of circulation. A notion of exclusion is therefore, inherent in the processing of discourse, as is evident from such available discourse of feminity, discourse of alternate sexuality, discourse of racism, discourse of class, and the one relevant in this context—the discourse of caste.

Feminism, alternate sexuality, race, class and their discourses are universal phenomena, whereas caste and its associated discourse are specific to India. Susan Bayly in *Caste, Society and Politics in India from the Eighteenth Century to the Modern Age* has very rightly observed: "nothing quite like the caste evolved in other parts of the world" (28). Division of the Hindu community into the four *varna* or castes, namely, *Brahmins*, *kshatriyas*, *vaishyas*, and *shudras* is a general form of organisation. The discrimination on the basis of *varna* or castes is an old practice in India, whereby the untouchables or *harijans* and especially the *dalits* are kept outside the ambit of the four-fold caste system. Dalit is not a caste and is known variously as exterior caste, outcaste, depressed class or scheduled caste (qtd. in Paswan et al. 11). *The Encyclopaedia of Dalits in India* lists caste system as "the main cause of disharmony and disunity in the community" (Paswan et al. 22). Initiatives were taken by reformers, especially during the pre-independence era by the likes of Mahatma Gandhi and Dr. B.R. Ambedkar to annihilate caste system. In the post-independence period, particularly after the 1990s, there has been a continuous and meticulous implementation of reservation quota in education and jobs to uplift the downtrodden. Yet, some parts of the country continue as domains of caste, with Brahmin-centred caste values being venerated as the core of human order and propriety, *dharma*. Natarajan paints a replica of such a stratified society in *No Onions Nor Garlic*, where the head of the English department at Chennai University, Professor Pattabhiram, popularly known as Professor Ram strives tirelessly to sustain the principle of caste hierarchy both inside and outside the university campus. In the professor's hands, caste becomes a site of power. In fact, caste politics is anticipated at the very beginning of the book with the staging of Shakespeare's play, *A Midsummer Night's Dream*. This play happened to be rewritten by Professor Ram, for the University fest. It was modified not to suit the needs of the stage, especially when it had come from the pen of the vindictive, a no nonsense 'no onions and garlic' Tamil Brahmin (the book draws its title from here), Professor Ram who was also the author of such a book as *Daddy What is the Significance of the Poonal and One Hundred Other Questions About Hinduism*. He remade the Shakespearean play to support the sanctimonious Hindu hierarchy. He knew very well that our attitude towards the castes is largely limited by 'knowledge'. Knowledge, as explored by Foucault in his collection of essays entitled *Power/Knowledge*, reiterate that, in order for something to be established as a fact/true, other equally valid statements have to be discredited or denied (qtd. in Mills 69). Only such statements are in circulation which underpin what is to be taken as 'common-sense knowledge' in society.

The saffron light came on stage when the play started to signify the hidden Hindu message of the play. The version enacted on the stage was quite contrary to what Shakespeare had originally intended when he wrote the play sometime between 1590 and 1596. The present performance at the Pantheon Theatre was replete with Professor Ram's interpolations; mainly pertaining to the question of the top-downwards model of the caste system in India. He rued the introduction of the Reservation Policy in government sectors. The treatment meted out to Dr. Laurentia Arul by Professor Ram and his Brahmin colleagues is amply suggestive here. Dr. Arul was a faculty of the same department as Professor Ram but she was a non-Brahmin and belonged to the reserved category. Hence, to humiliate her and to constantly make her aware of her low social status, the professor branded her as the 'low-caste Ambedkarite'. The constant bullying by her Brahmin colleagues cornered Dr. Arul. Professor Ram's anger against Dr. Arul actually reflected his stand against the Reservation Policy, which had advocated for more reservations in certain jobs for the backward castes and this provision, according to caste Hindus, in turn interfered with the recruitment procedures in Government institutions including universities. "In Professor Ram's opinion, Dr. Arul was not the most pernicious of the beasts that slouched towards Chennai University to be born. No, it was the Reservation Policy itself" (Natarajan 88). For him "the Reservation Policy was just snatching the curd-rice and mango pickle from the mouths of twice-born boys, especially Brahmins" (Natarajan 83). Efforts were taken not to produce the other side of 'knowledge' which were categorised as false statements. Each regime thus has its own regime of truth which is dispersed everywhere from the State or government to family, religious institutions and educational system.

"The system of education", as Foucault argues in "The order of discourse" (1981), "is a political way of maintaining or modifying the appropriation of discourses, along with the knowledges and powers which they carry" (64). The same idea is repeated by Pierre Bourdieu in *Reproduction in Education, Society and Culture*. Accordingly, the education system largely runs "to fulfil its social function of legitimating the dominant culture (124). The teachers are the vital 'agents', who have the prerogative to authoritatively decide the range of practices which will contribute to the institutionalisation of discourse of such dominant culture, class or caste. Thus, Professor Ram puts his body and soul to fight for the 'Future of Education'. According to him, it is a 'noble cause' to support the Brahmin students. He joins his Brahmin students in sweeping the streets, to show how the educated and the upper castes could not get any decent job after the Mandal Commission recommendations. He supervises PhDs only by Brahmin students. He even has 'special teaching methods' for lower caste students. Some of these methods were:

> Throwing their papers out of the classroom window, calling them names like dolt and nincompoop, which were not there in the attendance register, failing them in every examination, giving them his sincere blessing when they dropped out of the course, and treating them at all times as if they stood no higher than vermin in

> the evolutionary order.... Professor Ram treated these students in this manner because they came from backwater towns like Dindigul or Palayankottai, and had Christian names and non-Brahmin surnames, and were the same colour as soya sauce. (Natarajan 82)

Professor Ram was a shrewd man. He realized that power is present in human actions and not in the actions of institutions. He understood that merely attacking representative structures of the oppressed would not serve his purpose. Organisations or their buildings or statues of Dr. Ambedkar were all structures, which could be easily rebuilt after they were crushed. Hence, Professor Ram targeted the individuals, more specifically Dr. Arul. Dr. Arul had spearheaded the drive for the installation of the statue of Dr. Ambedkar in an educational institute, which as Professor Ram apprehended would become a cult figure for the student body of the reserved category students like the Students for Democracy. So, Professor Ram levelled the false allegation against Dr. Arul of besmirching his name by sticking notes containing offensive remarks on him, across the department. He even organised a march from the English department to the Vice Chancellor's bungalow, demanding the demolition of the Ambedkar statue. This undoubtedly contradicted Professor Ram's own desire to get a statue of Goddess Saraswati installed within the university campus for which he "would personally take responsibility...and pay half of its cost!" (Natarajan 197). His actions are in keeping with Foucault's observation in *Discipline and Punish* on educational institutions. Schools and universities in the West were established primarily to teach the students to be submissive and simultaneously to control their family. The seventeenth century Christian schools aimed not only to train docile children but also "to supervise the parents, to gain information as to their way of life, their resources, their piety, their morals. The school tends to constitute minute social observatories that penetrate even to the adults and exercise regular supervision over them" (Foucault 211).

Professor Ram and his marauding Brahmin workmates focussed less on the circulation of knowledge and more on the way certain types of knowledge were to be excluded, the rigorous process whereby the outcastes, be it the students, their parents or faculty, were to be brought into line with the type of knowledge considered to be 'academic' and 'true'. Thus, someone as educated as Professor Nagarajan of the same English department penned an article like 'Atrocities on Brahmins' where he talked about 'the sufferings of upper caste Indians who have to trust a Harijan doctor with their God-given bodies' (Natarajan 159). He criticized Dr. V.P. Singh, under whose Prime Ministership the 'affirmative action' mentioned in the Mandal Commission Report was publicized, for not going to the Public Health Centre but to the United Kingdom for his own treatment. All the high browed historians like Dr. Iyer "have observed, the 'so-called scheduled castes stomp with an upward motion and grind the upper castes into the stratosphere with an unprecedented gravity-defying aggression, a phenomenon to which we may apply the term "*uptrodedenness*"'" (83). "Ever since the Reservation Policy tied their hands", the Hindus, as Dr. Chaturvedi pointed out, were 'up- pressed' by the *harijans* in education, job and other sectors of life making them "accept...people who were not fit..." (193). The nefarious stance adopted by the Brahmins has drawn flak in Kancha Ilaih's "Merit of Reservation": "the same upper caste have never agitated against private medical, engineering and management colleges selling seats to the rich for money. An anti-caste policy like reservation is being projected as an anti-national policy" (2447).

This explains Professor Ram's interference in the interview for the Open Category post of Lecturer in Drama and Folklore at the university. An 'open category' post signified that candidate from any caste, creed or religion could apply. His student, Jiva who belonged to the scheduled caste community had also applied for the post. Professor Ram could not sit in the interview committee because his son, Sankarnarayanan or Chunky was one of the applicants. There were two female members in the committee, Dr. Arul and the University Grants Commission representative. Professor Ram hated the *shudras* and women, and persuaded others to select only the Brahmin faculty. When Professor Nagarajan told him about these two women, Professor Ram's anguish was clear: "these women...will form a fascist non-Brahmin caucus and try and push one of their people in, especially as they hate everything I stand for.... It will all become a matter of favouritism and caste-politics" (Natarajan 89-90). Consequently, he tried to manipulate the result of the panel even before the interview took place. He initially coaxed Jiva to abstain from the interview. Professor Ram held before her the bait of a confirmed job when the Reserved Category post came in: "..:the Reserved Category seat will be falling vacant six months from now.... It will be easier for me to guarantee you that job if you don't antagonize the department by competing for an Open Category post" (93). The professor even placed her under the 'invisible gaze' and reverted to threats: "Jiva, consider how you are placed in relation to your viva voce examination. I think a wise acceptance of the truth is better than an argument. You are going to need my recommendation" (94).

Despite all efforts, when Jiva still refused to withdraw her name from the interview, Professor Ram could only lament the absence of other high caste panellists. The absentee panellists like Professor Subbu was on a pilgrimage to Benaras; Professor Sambasivan had to be hospitalised for appendicitis; and most significantly Professor Venkat had been to a conference in America but missed his connecting flight in Frankfurt. "It is a tragedy", according to Professor Ram. "It is always our people who get invited to go to conferences abroad" (Natarajan 90). The poignant irony in this line is definitely an eye opener as it identifies the real beneficiaries of foreign conferences. However, at that instant it only serves to intensify the professor's despair as the chance for his son to get selected for the post seemed a distant possibility. Chunky, "according to reproduction theorists", as Bracha Alpert postulates in her article "Students' Resistance in the Classroom", is expected to "reproduce the ideology of dominant groups in society, their forms of knowledge" (351), carry forward the legacy of the upper caste dominance over the lower castes thereby maintaining the division of castes in the Indian society.

It cannot be ignored that wherever there are imbalances of power relations between groups of people or between institutions/states, there is bound to be a production of knowledge. This idea is echoed by Foucault as well in his essay entitled "Prison talk" (1980), where he states that "it is not possible for power to be exercised without knowledge, it is impossible for knowledge not to engender power" (52). He emphasises the way that knowledge is not dispassionate but an essential part of struggles over power. Foucault draws attention to the fact that, in producing knowledge, one also simultaneously stakes a claim to power. As a result, Professor Ram constantly manoeuvres to get his son selected for the post of lecturer in the university and himself elected as the president of the Association for Commonwealth Studies. He wanted to seal his son's as well as his place in that much coveted space of stalwarts who can speak authoritatively on castes. Professor Ram's action is in the line of Nietzschean thought of 'Will to Power', according to which, people first decide what they want and then they fit the facts to their aim. This at the same time also means that there are no absolute truths or objective knowledge.

Karuna Ahmad enunciates in "For Sociology in Teacher Education": "teachers are...under more public scrutiny than any other groups" (45). In addition to this, discourse which produces knowledge, as found in *The History of Sexuality*, Vol. I is, both "a hindrance, a stumbling block, a point of resistance and a starting point for an opposing strategy" (Foucault 100-01). Discourse, unlike the Marxist connotation of ideology, is both the means of persecution and the means of opposition. Moreover, discourse, truth and knowledge are intricately connected to power. And power, as Foucault had written in *Power/Knowledge* is "something which only functions in the form of a chain.... Power is employed and exercised through a net like organisation.... Individuals are the vehicles of power, not its points of application" (98). The marginalised therefore, in the academic sphere or in any institution have the potential to produce such information which can alter the status quo in the society. In *No Onions Nor Garlic* Professor Ram is then correct in observing the lower caste faculty members and students as non conformists to the long established system. Indeed, the Students for Democracy, a body comprising the lower caste students in Chennai University constantly toils towards erasing the facile Hindu way of life. The fact that "dalit studies are getting a lot of recognition these days" (Natarajan 277) distinctly highlights that, due to institutionalised imbalances in power relations between the upper castes and the oppressed, information is produced about the 'dalits' and few on the Hindu upper castes; thus many researches and plenty of books on the 'dalit' subject are to be found in universities and libraries. Nevertheless, "all that caste-oppression stuff is history. The tables are pretty much turned now" (37). The entire Brahmin faculty and the students of the university rallied against the consecration of the statue of Dr. Ambedkar within the campus, whereas the reserved category students and the faculty came up with a series of rhetorical questions on 'hero-worship', 'independence' and 'the news about Gujarat' to justify the installation of the same. The Students for Democracy also organised an outrage against the exorbitant registration fee demanded to attend the Association of Commonwealth Studies conference convened by Professor Ram. A group of 'registration-dodgers' flouted the basic rule of the conference and sat in the sessions with placards which made a suggestion, "free discussion, not fee collection" (273). Resistance is after all, an act of liberation when power is viewed as domination.

A whole seemingly self-evident system of silencing and compelling to speak, of commenting on and assessing a work in relation to fixed parameters exists, which in turn leads to the mapping out of power relations between lecturers and students. This is very closely related to what Professor Nagarajan asserts, though in Sanskrit, "*Guru saakshaath parabrahma*.... The teacher is equal to the ah-Over-Soul" (Natarajan 91). The effect of this power is that Professor Ram "was indeed a dead ringer for the Over-Soul" (91), who was always keen to cash in the sacredness of the teacher-student relationship. Hence, Shastri despite working towards his PhD under the supervision of Professor Ram could not submit his thesis in fourteen long years. Shastri had written eight drafts of his thesis but each got rejected without being properly checked:

> The first draft of my thesis was 187 pages. The second draft was 231 pages, the third, 197, the fourth, 193, the fifth, 204, the sixth, 214, the seventh, 216, and the eighth, 220 exactly.... I have written eight drafts of my thesis titled "Hedgerows, Hardly Hedgerows: Dwarf Plants and Crotons in Wordsworth's Poetry". This is amounting to a total of 1,662 pages. (301)

As mentioned in "For Sociology in Teacher Education", "teachers are in particularly sensitive relation to the community" (Ahmad 45) and Professor Ram worked towards purging the "mean corridors of academe" (Natarajan 84) of the evils brought by the scheduled castes and scheduled tribes faculty members and students. The professor, therefore, required someone trust worthy to aid him realize his goal, write posters, hold demonstrations and Shastri was the best option available. Over the years Shastri had naturally become the professor's "full-time chamcha and right-hand man" (18). Apparently, he was the student editor of *The Brahmasatra* and the unanimously elected president of the Anti-Reservation Society of Egmore but in reality, Shastri was no better than an office-bearer exploited by the professor. The researcher's future rested within the thesis supervisor's control and this gave the professor licence to exercise power over Shastri. Frustration drove Shastri to stick malicious notes on Professor Ram anonymously across the walls of the department in order to teach him a lesson:

> Professor (Dickface) Ram invites a dead theorist called *Foucault* to his conference. He just takes all the conference money to get his daughter married. He should be *throne* in the sea, and we should get a new Head for the English Department.... (291)

There is a general perception that in educational institutes, students retorting to teachers or resisting the authority of teachers is seen as aberrant, or potentially disruptive of the status quo. Nevertheless, Shastri paves the way to critique the power wielded by the dominant, that is, the professors and teachers, even if it means back stabbing.

Foucault explained this kind of resistance against the dominant class in *Power/Knowledge* as "a matter rather of establishing the positions occupied and modes of actions used by each of the forces at work, the possibilities of resistance and counter-attack on either side" (163-64). Hence, even Sundar, another Brahmin scholar working with Professor Ram, when appointed against his wishes to assist Shastri in safeguarding the principles of Brahmin students and denouncing the commemoration of the Ambedkar statue within the university campus, he assumed the role of the whistleblower. Sundar joined the oppressed students in their fight for equality with other students from the unreserved category. In addition to this, he even typed the 'protest letter' for the Students for Democracy when they decided to march for providing justice to the wronged Dr. Arul. Students in general therefore, behave quite differently when out of their teacher's presence. They jeer at their teachers, tell stories of ways in which the powerful persons will be mortified and invent demeaning nicknames as happens in the case of the new literary criticism lecturer in the English department. The lady, who was a fresh out of the University of California at Berkeley, had the habit of saying that things were 'always already'. The students could not fathom why things were 'always already'. So, they forgot her real name which was Kalpana Kamath and called her Always Already instead. It is clearly noticeable that the behaviours of both the powerful and the powerless are regulated within the power relation.

Power relations however, "...are multiple; they have different forms", as Foucault states in an interview entitled "Critical theory/intellectual theory" (qtd. in Mills 35). They can be at work within an institution or an administration or in family relations specifically in the relation between man and woman. In *No Onions Nor Garlic* the most striking model of such a relation between the two sexes and power is perceived in the marriage of the Rams'. Professor Ram by virtue of being a conservative Tamil Brahmin had devoted an entire chapter under the heading "Daddy, What is the Role of Women in Hindu tradition?" in the only book which he had written in his lifetime, to discuss the issues pertaining to the conduct of women both within the family and outside it. He even modified the Shakespearean drama *A Midsummer Night's Dream* to fit in his ideas on women, "especially when Oberon began to say acid things about the role of woman in Hindu society" (Natarajan 32). Interestingly, it is not the 'Hindu society' or India at large alone which charts out the role of women, but as Robert Greene's study observes women were treated as sub-ordinates in every field across the globe. Greene writes in *The Art of Seduction: 24 Laws of Persuasion*, "thousands of years ago, power was mostly gained through physical violence and maintained with brute strength. There was little need for subtlety—a king or emperor had to be merciless. Only a select few had power, but no one suffered under this scheme of things more than women" (xix).

This is distinctly perceptible from the caustic remarks of Professor Ram in the guise of Oberon which were primarily directed against the lower caste women of the University, like Dr. Arul, for whom he had absolutely no respect. "You know Laurentia's face? I have met fire-extinguishers with more sex appeal" (Natarajan 87). Speaking about the fair sex is in reality a way of simultaneously producing and controlling it and this is far more marked in familial relationships. Nevertheless, the professor's remark raises an important question on the power-gender-caste nexus. Accordingly, Uma Chakravarti in "Conceptualising Brahmanical Patriarchy in Early India: Gender, Caste, Class and State" states, "caste hierarchy and gender hierarchy are the principles of the brahmanical social order" (579).

It is intrinsic for Professor Ram to dictate the terms of marriage to his wife. His notion of marriage was founded on the old Hindu order, according to which his own marriage to Mrs. Ram had entered that unusual stage whereby "they just moulted their special clothes without looking at each other and fell into their separate beds" and Mrs. Ram too "realized that the entry into sannyaasan would be marked by the complete cessation of the old rumpy-pumpy. She truly understood, then, that the Hindu wife's duty was to curb lustful propensities and promote universal harmony" (Natarajan 138). Chakravarti explains Mrs. Ram's behaviour in terms of the ideology of 'pativrata' or 'stridharma' which is accepted wholeheartedly by women in general. Women, as exemplified by Mrs. Ram motivated by the ideology of 'stridharma' strive towards fulfilling the expectations of their husbands. When Professor Ram had nightmares, it was presumed that the first duty of the Hindu wife was to roll out of her single bed and bring him a tumbler full of warm milk to soothe him, and the second duty was to massage her husband's legs, not lustfully but impersonally, until he fell asleep again. Interestingly, Foucault uncovered this ideology of 'pativrata' or 'stridharma'. He opined that such ideology is a device of patriarchy to exercise power over women. It subjects the person to 'invisible gaze' and subsequently changes the behaviour of the person, here, Mrs. Ram, who internalizing such ideology becomes a 'self-monitoring' agent and in due course of time also makes it appear as a 'normal' phenomenon. Chakravarti reinforces Foucault's explanation in her article, "Conceptualising Brahmanical Patriarchy in Early India: Gender, Caste, Class and State":

> Pativrata, the ideological 'purdah' of the Hindu women was...the mask by which the hierarchical and inegalitarian structure of the social order was reproduced.... The actual mechanisms and institutions of control over women's sexuality, and the subordination of women, was...completely invisibilised and with it patriarchy was firmly established as an ideology since it was "naturalised". (583)

Foucault continued with his insight on gender as power structure in *The History of Sexuality*, Vol. I. He discusses in this book, where "a multiplication of discourses concerning sex in the field of exercise of power" (18) determine the category 'women', it can hardly be imagined that somebody, especially a girl can have a different sexual orientation other than being heterosexual. Consequently, when it was disclosed that the Rams' daughter, Jayanthi was a lesbian and in a relationship with a Canadian blonde, Caroline, even planning to marry her, Jayanthi's parents had no other option but to disown their only daughter. Not only the choice of orientation, in a society which allows only men to serve as power structures and police the behaviour of women, the simple wish to marry a man of one's own liking is also a matter of great consternation. Probably this is the reason why Sundar's sister, Uma's desire to wait for someone who would love her for what she is and whom she could equally love is labelled as being too romantic and film like. On the other hand, a 'tubbier' divorcee who is "beginning to be Muruga!—*bald*" (Natarajan 115) is considered a much more socially viable match for the dark complexioned, twenty-seven-year-old Uma.

Women are circumscribed within the power structures but individuals, be it man or woman, should not be simply seen as the recipients of power. If they are the place where power is enacted then they are also the place where power is resisted. The same idea is restated in the works of Judith Butler, who having been influenced by Foucault's concern with the materiality of power relations at a local level, too tries to assume that power is not simply located in institutions. She emphasises that sex and gender are the results of discourse and law but at the same time insists on the possibilities for growth and subversion from within existing discursive structures, more so since no position can be taken up outside the checks imposed by power structures (qtd. in Salih 50).

'Resistance' can be converted to 'power' by neutralising the impact of the 'invisible gaze' of different power structures like poverty, shame, death, caste, class, religion, family or gender. The selection of Dr. Arul to the post of the president of the Association of Commonwealth Studies for a term of three years in Professor Ram's place is a direction towards this change. Moreover, Jayanthi continues her affair with a girl and sticks to her decision of marrying the same sex despite being forsaken by her parents. Uma too secretly marries the man she loves. However, the real inversion of the order takes place after it is disclosed that Professor Ram is actually the son of a low caste dancing girl, the brother of Dr. Arul, in short, not a true born Brahmin. A behavioural change ensues in Mrs. Ram. Chakravarti is accurate when she says: "the upper caste women is the object of moral panic. Through the recalcitrance of women the established property and status order can be subverted" (579-80). As such, Mrs. Ram continued to perform the duties of a Hindu wife but knowing that her husband is 'fifty per cent low-caste', her visits to the god man, Sri Sri Sri Sastrigal "to get herself purified up" became more frequent. Professor Ram's personal life was all shot to pieces, with Mrs. Ram frequently reminding him that she had "married beneath her". Professor Ram was relegated to an absolute nothing. He had to "cook, and wash the silver tumblers he drinks out of, and make the beds, and iron his shirts, all by himself" (Natarajan 325). Moving away from the family life to the professional space, Professor Ram received a setback there too. He was robbed of his position as the head of the department. A new head, a Brahmin though, was appointed. However, Professor Ram was isolated by his Brahmin compatriots. A scheduled caste student was chosen to fill the Open Category post for lecturer. University culture showed the signs of being genuinely egalitarian, something which was unthinkable during Professor Ram's tenure as the head of the department.

The ending of *No Onions Nor Garlic* with its confusions, squabbles and the denigration of Professor Ram is almost burlesque. It is rib tickling but at the same time it has overtones of bitterness. The bitterness explored in this campus novel is a consequence of play of power relations. It may appear exaggerated; nevertheless, it is healthier and wiser not to cherish idyllic fantasies about the academic world and the academicians inhabiting that world. For their occupants possess that knowledge which does not emerge from scholarly study alone rather, is produced in such ways and maintained in circulation in societies through the operation of various institutions and practices that it becomes the tool in the hands of interest groups. This reveals the interconnectedness of knowledge and discourse; and knowledge, discourse and power. Power is ubiquitous and as such power is evident in every interaction. Interestingly, as is clear from the analysis of the relationships between teacher and student, high caste and low caste, and both the sexes in *No Onions Nor Garlic*, it is very difficult to identify who is exercising power because the real exerciser remains invisible. The succinct appraisal of the power relations in *No Onions Nor Garlic* explains the vital question about the automatic functioning of the hierarchical set up in a professor-student relationship, caste system and gender. The elucidations from the novel discover not only the ways of resistance, or the major ways of exercising power and countering power with 'artificial power' but also points out the problems of the individuals involved in power relations.

WORKS CITED

Ahmad, Karuna. "For Sociology in Teacher Education." *Themes in Sociology of Education*. Ed. R. Indira. Vol. 5. New Delhi: Sage, 2012: 42-55.

Alpert, Bracha. "Students' Resistance in the Classroom." *Anthropology of Education Quaterly* 22. 4 (Dec. 1991): 350-66. *JSTOR*. Web. 4 Apr. 2013. http://www.jstor.org/stable/3195659

Baldick, Chris. *The Concise Oxford Dictionary of Literary Terms*. Oxford: Oxford UP, 1990.

Bayly, Susan. *Caste, Society and Politics in India from the Eighteenth Century to the Modern Age*. Cambridge: Cambridge UP, 1999.

Bordieu, Pierre, and Jean-Claude Passerson. *Reproduction in Education, Society and Culture*. Trans. Richard Nice. London: Sage Publications, 1990.

Chakravarti, Uma. "Conceptualising Brahmanical Patriarchy in Early India: Gender, Caste, Class and State." *Economic and Political Weekly* 28. 14 (1993): 579-85.

Foucault, Michel. *Power/Knowledge: Selected Interviews and Other Writings, 1972-1977*. Trans. Colin Gordon, Leo Marshall, John Mepham, and KateSoper. Ed. Colin Gordon. New York: Pantheon, 1980.

——. "Prison talk." Trans. Colin Gordon, Leo Marshall, John Mepham, and KateSoper. *Power/Knowledge: Selected Interviews and Other Writings, 1972-1977*. Ed. Colin Gordon. New York: Pantheon, 1980: 37-54.

——. "The order of discourse." *Untying the Text: A Post-structuralist Reader*. Ed. Robert J.C. Young. London: Routledge and Kegan Paul, 1981: 48-79.

——. *The Archaeology of Knowledge*. Trans. A.M. Sheridan Smith. London: Routledge, 1972.

——. *The History of Sexuality,* Vol. I: *An Introduction*. Trans. Robert Hurley. Harmondsworth: Penguin, 1978.

Greene, Robert. *The Art of Seduction: 24 Laws of Persuasion*. New York: Viking Penguin, 2001.

Ilaiah, Kancha. "Merit of Reservations." *Economic and Political Weekly* 41. 24 (June 17, 2006): 2447-49.

Mills, Sara. *Michel Foucault*. London: Routledge, 2003.

Natarajan, Srividya. *No Onion, Nor Garlic*. New Delhi: Penguin, 2006.

Paswan, Sanjay, and Paramanshi Jaideva, eds. *Encyclopaedia of Dalits in India*. Delhi: Kalpaz Publication, 2004.

Salih, Sarah. *Judith Butler*. London: Routledge, 2002.

Showalter, Elaine. *Faculty Towers: The Academic Novel and its Discontents*. Philadelphia: University of Pennsylvania Press, 2005.

Shridevi, P.G. "The Origin and Development of Campus Novels in Indian English Literature." *The Indian Review of World Literature in English* (*IRWLE*) 7. 2 (2011): 1-9. *Worldlitonline.* Web. 18 Jan. 2013. http://worldlitonline.net/the-origin-and-development.pdf

White, Edward, and David Widger, prods. *Leviathan*. By Thomas Hobbes. 1651. *Gutenberg*. N.p. 11 Oct. 2009. Web. 19 Feb. 2015. http://www.gutenberg.org/files/3207/3207-h/3207-h.htm

❑❑❑

Literary-Cultural Conversations with Kiran Nagarkar on the Art of the Indian Writer

RAMONA L. CECIU

RLC: Dear writer Kiran Nagarkar, allow me to say that I consider your fiction to be among the most valuable literary creations of contemporary India, so I have included your fiction in my doctoral research, whose focus forms the basis of our conversation. Broadly speaking how would you define your style of writing and what is your creed as an author? It is maybe difficult to speak about one's own writing, but you may see it as an exercise in self-reflectivity.

KN: For me the subject dictates my style and the form. I maintain this very strongly. I have to add that one of the things that are important to me is the transparency of language. I do not like to use highly complicated or obfuscating language. I believe that the immediate function of fiction is to entertain readers. My writing hopefully has subterranean levels, implications and meanings but my first priority is to grip the interest of the reader.

I don't care too much for a creed or manifesto but I talk about what I see as the role of the artist in the 21st century in my essay, *Shiva's Blue Throat*. I had no idea that I would one day get around to writing such an essay. What I deal with in it are my options, aspirations and beliefs as a writer. I've always thought that I should not have overt messages in my writing. But I broke my own injunction in my play *Bedtime Story*. It has a powerful, overt message; maybe that's why it has not been published yet. Anyway I must emphasize that I believe in storytelling, and in this sense my role models are those authors who wrote the *Mahabharata*, *Iliad* and other epics. Their appeal has lasted for millennia and they are still going strong.

Over the last few decades I have found that many critics look down on 'plot'. The assumption is that plot is the hallmark of pulp in direct contrast to the exploration of character which is said to be the hallmark of literature. This is a bogus polarization and counter-productive. Plot and character, as far as I am concerned are intimately and inseparably connected. The one throws light on the other and vice versa. Take a random instance like Graham Greene's *Heart of the Matter.* The protagonist Major Scobie would never have run into the nineteen-year old widow, Helen Rolt if there had been no shipwreck and the story would have gone nowhere. It is the plot which reveals the depths of Scobie's predicament and ultimate tragedy. Of course, whether the plot is merely a device to push the story forward or is a means to develop and instill a variety of nuances in the characters and thus bring forth their complexity will depend entirely on the author. But as far as I am concerned the plot throws light on a character's inner mechanisms and mindset. But in parallel the character of a character is also what dictates the plot. In *Ravan and Eddie,* for instance Ravan and his mother Parvati discover one day that his father Shankar-rao has brought over a woman called Lalee who he claims is his sister. Both mother and son soon realize that the so-called sister is Shankar-rao's mistress. It is indeed an existential crisis for Ravan and Parvati since Lalee is intent on taking over their home. They both are forced to find their own ways to get rid of the outsider. Parvati employs sex and a dire threat to bring her husband in line. Ravan on the other hand exploits his reputation for black magic to blackmail Lalee into leaving his home.

Some people have criticized me for writing about sex explicitly. I repeat that it is the content that dictates my style. In my books, like *Ravan and Eddie*, *Seven Sixes are Forty-Three*, and in its sequel, *The Extras* and even *Cuckold*, there may be some passages which are explicit, but in *God's Little Soldier* I do not deal with sex at all. And that is because the book does not call for it. These examples explain how I try to follow my own dictum that the subject dictates my style in a particular book.

RLC: This is like lived reality, because in many ways the events and experiences we have dictate our evolution in life and the paths we take. It is the story of Ravan and Eddie and their evolution too. Besides, to go to my next point, please tell me—in your view, how important is the language in which a writer writes—how important is it for the narrative and for the author? I ask this in the light of certain claims that Indian writing in English is not 'truly Indian'. I do not agree with such claims and I certainly argue against such positions, but they exist. So, how imperative is the language in which a writer writes?

KN: Let me start with a preamble. My mother-tongue is Marathi, but then because of a change of circumstances, I was forced to switch to English. I find that some people speak in Marathi and are against their children going to English schools, while others want their children to go only to English medium schools. They are all aware that English is necessary because whether they like it or not, if they want their children to go abroad to study or get good jobs, English is a must. But the question I would like to ask is: 'If you want the best for your children, and you give them English education, then how come the mother-tongue is not among the best things for your child?' Again I don't see English and the mother tongue as mutually incompatible at all. The fact is that this purported dichotomy is a hoax. Over the years I have become a strong advocate of learning any language that is a child's mother-tongue while I think that the more languages you know the richer you are. Oddly enough I discuss the problem of languages in an aside or rumination in *Ravan and Eddie*. I wrote my first novel and a play in Marathi by sheer accident, and I consider it truly unfortunate that I can write *only* in two languages and not more, but it's rather late in the day to master any other languages, whether Indian or foreign.

RLC: After so many years of living in India, I certainly can say that there is no single definition of Indian 'culture' or the 'Indian Self,' but an infinite multiplicity. However, let's try to think of Indian culture as including three important dimensions; one *material*, one *social* and one *spiritual*. How do you perceive the dynamics and relations between these three dimensions in contemporary India from your position as an Indian, living in and writing about India? Also, what is your evaluation of this dynamic from the perspective of power relations (or hierarchy) at work in Indian society, and how do you think it affects the Indian psyche?

KN: The formative influences in my life and thinking can be traced to four sources: (1) I was born almost on the cusp of the Indian freedom struggle when the figures of Gandhi, Nehru, Patel, Abul Kalam Azad and other freedom fighters were a major presence in our society and the way we thought about the world. (2) The influence of the Brahmo Samaj and the reform movements in Maharashtra and Bengal. (3) The rapid slide into corruption and bureaucratic red tape from the 1960's; and (4) the discovery of the free-market economy and the worship of mammon from the mid-1990s.

After we got Independence, it was natural to expect that idealism and ideals like honesty, integrity, service to the people and nation-building would be of primary importance. In terms of my later writing, the institutions of the chawls, not to mention the slums and the footpath dwellings, I took it for granted that our own government would, over a period of time, replace these awful warrens with decent, airy and economical but sensibly designed self-sufficient dwellings because we cared for the people who lived there and we thought that they too deserved the dignity that is the due of any human being, rich or poor. Today, unfortunately, the material, the spiritual and the social coalesce into one single theology and that is 'money'. Of course there are some exceptions, no doubt about that, but at the present the prevalent trend is capitalism, the power of money, greed and corruption. We are in a way extremely monogamous and the marriage we have undertaken in every aspect of life is with money. Nearly everyone with few honorable exceptions has accepted these 'values' so that it's hard to imagine what the future of our society with its extremes will be.

RLC: The problem is that the discrepancy between the rich and the poor is very wide in Indian society, and this appears in your novel *Ravan and Eddie* too. This novel along with *The Extras*, but also *Seven Sixes are Forty Three* (*Saat Sakkam Trechalis*), reveal multiple facets of Mumbai, with its chawls in contrast to the posh areas, with its people of different backgrounds, religions, languages and mores. Each facet is probably a mixture of real and fictitious elements. In Indian society as such the discrepancy between the rich and the poor is extremely wide, and in many ways literature has the capacity to signal such social issues. Because you live in Mumbai and your relation with the city must be quite intimate, tell me please what is in your view the way out for the people who live in such utter poverty just beside luxurious buildings and rich people? Do you think (or do you have any feedback) that your works can trigger awareness and action against such problems? What is the *story behind* the *story* of young people like Ravan and Eddie in contemporary times? What can they expect of life?

KN: If they had a choice no self-respecting Indian with a cushy job with Morgan Stanley or one of the investment firms would want to see or run into the poor. They are an eye-sore. If only they would just disappear from sight. Most lavish advertisements, at least in Mumbai, show high-rise buildings, luxury spaces, new walled fortresses, which cosset you and yours from that disease called poverty. Unfortunately, the rich and the super-rich in these luxury buildings still need the slums next door, because who's going to do the washing, the sweeping, and the cooking? Add to that, let's not forget the Porsche and the BMW have to be washed and someone has to drive the sahib to work and memsahib to the kitty party. So the poor are wanted for limited and specific purposes.

One of the criticisms of *The Extras* was that it ends on a feel-good note as if the poor are either incapable of breaking through the barrier of poverty or worse should know their place in life and don't deserve anything better. I think Ravan and Eddie go through a nightmarish odyssey to just survive, even as adults. For some critics it would have made aesthetic sense if they had not made good at the end. But I do believe that once in a very rare while, some dreams do come true. The hard-working, the talented can occasionally make good on their own steam and not because the script-writer decided to have a happy ending. Didn't the freedom struggle end on a happy note! Imagine Gandhiji was able to attract not only the finest intellectuals but the poorest and most depressed in the country and they all fought together, something which is inconceivable today. If that is not a happy ending, I don't know what is, regardless of what we did with it.

RLC: Yes, Mahatma Gandhi had great ideals and many of his principles could take effect in real life, but somehow many of his principles have remained theoretical, people do not apply them. I have in mind for instance the constant discrimination that still exists in different degrees in terms of caste and class, or in terms of the Muslim-Hindu distinctions, which are entrenched in the Indian psyche, and even though some people would openly state that there are no such distinctions anymore in India, their own behavior and language betray a different reality. What do you feel about the, what may be called, 'failure' of Gandhian spirit or the viability of his principles in today's world? My focus is on the disjuncture that often appears between *speaking* about the Gandhian ideals and *doing* exactly the opposite in practical life.

KN: To understand what the 'failure' of the Gandhian spirit means one needs to know Gandhian philosophy, and as far as I can see, people do not really know it and have absolutely no interest in anything to do with Gandhi. For some time I have had an intense desire to make a large poster and plaster it all over the place. The poster will show the silhouette of a man with his back to the viewer. He's wearing a short dhoti, thin-rimmed spectacles and walking with a stick. The headline will say: 'Has anyone seen this man?' And the copy below will say: "He has been missing for over sixty years now. How can a whole nation forget its father, a man who led the most unique freedom struggle in the world and helped us win independence? You hear about him for two minutes on the 2nd of October and the 30th of January and then he's 'disappeared' and forgotten all over again."

We have long since erased all traces of the man. Along with Nehru, many today consider him a villain. People abroad have often accused me of hero-worshipping Gandhiji. The pre-condition of hero-worship is that it is uncritical and does not do justice to the person. Respect on the other hand will come only if you are able to appraise and evaluate a person without prejudice and without idolizing him. In short, with a level head. The first thing one needs to understand is that Gandhi and Nehru were human beings, not divine beings. And like all human beings they were flawed but unlike most human beings their achievements were exceptional. They cared deeply for their fellow human beings and fought for the fundamental rights of all humanity. We have either made them the bad guys or dismissed them as irrelevant. For instance many people consider Gandhi responsible for the Partition; these people don't even know their own history. We are perpetually speaking about Indian spirituality, but people rarely admit that ours is now more a monetary spirituality. There is hardly any talk about Gandhiji, and when there is talk about him, often it conceals certain hypocritical attitudes.

This issue is related to the previous one. That disjuncture is very clear, and I think it is there because we have become so utterly self-centered. There is nothing beyond *oneself*. If you read the writings of the sociologist Oscar Lewis who worked in Mexico and even in India, being primarily concerned with the poor; if you read his major thesis about the *Culture of Poverty*, which says that 'those who are extremely poor have no notion of tomorrow and deferred pleasure', then you understand something at the very heart of poverty. Let me take an example: if there is a Muslim *dargah* at a peer or a saint's tomb, food will often be served free to the poor on the saint's birthday. What happens then is that the poor will eat all that is served even when their appetite has been sated quite some time earlier. They do not keep anything aside for two reasons, they have no fridge and besides they don't know when their next meal will be. For the poor there is no notion of deferred pleasure in the future, no tomorrow. There is only the 'just now' and nothing else.

Now to make my point, I think that in the contemporary world, ironically it is the rich who have no sense of tomorrow. Yes, they do work hard, some cheat and use all kinds of underhand methods to amass a fortune to leave to their children but they cannot even see that that money may prove to be utterly useless if the fate of our planet, or rather of mankind on this planet is in extremely grievous danger and there may not be a future or tomorrow. So what will they leave for the coming generations? This contradiction and extreme short-sightedness affects most of the world's leadership and of course the super-rich like the Koch brothers and the heads of Goldman Sachs and Morgan Stanley.

RLC: Indeed, I do agree with you. And these discrepancies between rich and poor appear at several points throughout your fiction. Your recent novel *God's Little Soldier*—definitely not what some reviewer called "an act of literary terrorism"—deals among other things with the various extremes that a human being may reach through a lifetime according to different events that influence the person. It is obvious that Zia–Lucens–Tejas, like many people in the lived real world, needs to reach the point of death to understand that life itself is the most precious divine gift and that is what he should have treasured and nothing else—not the identities, or religions or labels he has constantly hanged on to. Do you feel that readers truly understand the most valuable points you emphasize in this novel? To what extent do you think that contemporary readers read responsibly, that is, by learning something of what they read and try to integrate that learning in their life? Regarding this novel in fact I also wonder, why have you made Zia a Muslim Indian, and not a Hindu?

KN: I had hoped that *God's Little Soldier* would have an impact all over the world because of its thematic significance and the fact that there are few non-thrillers written on the extremely important subject of extremism-terrorism of all hues, but barring Germany, I don't think it made an impression anywhere else. When we in India speak about Islamic culture, we know it is central to Indian culture. Forgive an unnecessary aside, but I must say that it intrigues and bothers me no end that Muslim men, who may have at the most beards as identifying marks, won't tell their women that they too are entitled to air and light as much as they are and do not need to wear the claustrophobic *boorkha*. I chose a Muslim family as the center of my novel because more often than not, Muslims across the world are seen to be bigoted and fanatical. Where do people get such notions, I don't know. I wanted to get this across—that Islam is not one color but like any culture and religion, multi-hued. And so the Khan family at the centre of the novel is supremely cultured. Yes, Zia is an extremist, but that is not the doing of his family. Even though his aunt is seen as a negative motivating agent by many, I think she is a simple woman and when she wants him to be a 'good Muslim' I do not think she has the remotest idea of turning him into an extremist-terrorist.

RLC: But from the psychological perspective it is important to note the role of the aunt, Zubeida, in his development. Children acquire habits and stereotypes from the parents, which they transmit further, to those around them; Zubeida's attitudes and the way she inculcates many ideas in Zia's mind, contribute largely to what he becomes. She is instrumental in the making of Zia as an adult. Apart from Zia's jealousy towards his brother, Amanat, the only other important factor in his life is Zubeida's love and attention. I consider of crucial significance, for instance, the moment when Zia takes a knife and goes to stab the poor street-dog fed by the pan-seller, Paanwalla Bajrang, because he had heard his aunt saying—"If only someone would rid us of these Hindu dogs...." Of course Zubeida was ignorant about the seriousness and incorrectness of her statement, but Zia's subsequent behavior demonstrates the impact language has on the human mind and its potential for harm, as well as the possible effects even random remarks adults make may have on children's mindsets. Zubeida was herself a victim of her own ignorance; she had a limited worldview which she imposed indirectly or directly on Zia.

KN: Well, you are right. Zia is constantly trying to live up to what he thinks Zubeida expects of him. But in the family there are other members, there is Abaajan, Ammijan, and there are the family friends, Dr. Patwardhan and his daughter, who all seem to have open, tolerant ways of looking at life. At the same time there is something in Zia which tends towards extreme views and makes him a soft target for religious fanaticism which one identifies in his aunt. For me Zia was that rare being in our mammon-besotted culture, he was an idealist. And that made him special for me. Unfortunately like so many idealists, he begins to believe that since his goals and objectives are honorable or noble, the end justifies the means. Shashi Tharoor saw the book as a study in terrorism and when he wrote a review of the novel, he was surprised that terrorism occupied only ten pages of the book. I wasn't however, writing a book about terrorism, but about extremism.

I am glad that you mentioned the dog episode, and in response to your question about responsible reading, I must tell you that most readers elide over that brief but crucial moment. As in *Ravan and Eddie*, Ravan grasps only that he has killed Eddie's father. He is not able to ask himself—'What nonsense is this? I didn't lead Victor Coutinho on. It was the exact opposite'; because he was only one year old when Eddie's father died saving Ravan. But there's worse to come: when Ravan tries to enroll members for the extremist Hindu organization called the Sangh, one of his friend's fathers gives Ravan hell and tells him that he and his ilk were responsible for the murder of Gandhiji. This revelation makes things much worse, he's now a double murderer. And imagine, the second murder is that of the Farther of the Nation. On the one hand it's funny, but from the child's point of view it signifies something terrible. That is why the dog scene, the perfume-shop related events, are crucial in *God's Little Soldier*.

RLC: Well, I have noticed them and I have examined them at different points in detail in my work.

KN: I am so glad. I do believe that comedy can be as serious as serious or tragic novels, but *God's Little Soldier*, I think, has one underlying theme for me. I suspect you know the lines….

RLC: I do know them: "There's only one God and Her name is Life"….

KN: Yes. So you see, if people cannot even grasp the importance of those lines, then I have failed. Hardly anybody applies Gandhian principles today. Gandhiji's notion of 'village culture' is so relevant to what we are doing to the planet at this moment and yet we ignore his views and philosophy.

RLC: I believe that even if there is just one reader who reads responsibly, that really matters. In my view that is imperative, and I often wonder—'how responsibly readers read?!' The word 'responsibly' implies the fact of really understanding what they read, how long do they think about what they have read, also how they integrate what they have read into their own life—because in my opinion this is how a reader needs to read literature. However, this does not always happen and this may be the trouble with the act, or practice of reading.

KN: I find my views resonating to your take on reading. And I am grateful that you have read my books so carefully.

RLC: I do relate to your writing and I agree with many of your views. Maybe some people are nervous to see how voluminous *God's Little Soldier* is. But if a reader wants to read and comprehend a literary work then it does not matter if the book has 100 or 400 pages. Anyway, I think it is more important to have fewer but 'true' readers, 'quality readers' (those who read your books carefully, deeply, responsibly) than more 'superficial readers'—those who read quickly and look only for some aspects of your books.

KN: Yes, I take your point.

RLC: *Ravan and Eddie* and, even more, *The Extras* are wonderful portrayals of the Bollywood factory of films and stardom, revealing both the light and the dark spaces of this immense living theatre. Stars live as long as they are in the limelight; the public adoration is the air they need to exist. And the two protagonists, extremely lovable in their innocence, experience this world of light from its *margins*. For those who have no connection with the film industry all seems beautiful, people all over the world are fans of Indian films, and mostly these fans do not question the actual realities behind the surface of glamour. And your fiction does exactly that: questions and unravels certain realities beyond/behind the camera. The first question in this context is: What is your relation with Indian films? The second question: How would you characterize the opposition between the Bollywood style of life—as it happens in reality and on the screen—and the style of life of the rest of Indians, in terms of openness towards dress codes, human inter-relations and so on? Because it is this opposition that makes youths like Ravan and Eddie dream about becoming stars.

KN: Though Bollywood films have a connection with my life, that occurred very late. Odd as it may sound I was not fond of Bollywood movies. What had hooked me from childhood were not the films, but the music. Music from the films of the 1950s and 1960s for instance was as close to immortality as it is possible for a three-and-a half-minute recording. Now you might tell me that this is pure nostalgia, and I am romanticizing but I believe that many of the lyric-writers and music directors of those times were touched by genius. There were an extraordinary variety of styles of music, light, semi-classical or hard-core classical music, or jazzed up sound tracks because of foreign influences. There was a remarkable, frankly astounding variety of music and music directors then right up to around 2007. Now it's mostly Punjabi film music.... As you know, I am from Maharashtra, and Maharashtrians by and large are supposed to be traditional and frugal people. If you went to a Maharashtrian wedding in those days, the close friends and relatives would be given a good meal to celebrate the wedding, which lasted for one day, but in the evening—because the middle class couldn't afford it, all you were offered was a soft drink or at the most a plate of ice-cream; this was due to both financial restrictions and also because of the Maharashtrian temperament. But all that has undergone major changes in the last few years.

Even a Maharashtrian wedding can go on for two or three days now. We follow the Punjabi model as popularized by Hindi films like *Hum Aapke Hai Kaun*. (Believe it or not the interior of the Liberty cinema hall was lit up as a wedding hall for this movie.) The Maharashtrian wedding has changed beyond recognition. It now allots one day to the *haldi* ceremony where the bride will be given the turmeric treatment and bathed; the next evening will be devoted to *sangeet*, or film and pop music with dancing where a good time is supposed to be had by everybody. The wedding with all the religious ceremonies will occupy the third day and the big reception will be either on that evening or the next day. And the dinner will offer a choice of eight or nine varieties of cuisine. Now if you go to such a wedding, which is elaborate and hugely expensive you will instantly grasp that the role model here is the Bollywood movies and the effect they have now on our daily lives.

Since we are on the subject of food, it's quite ironic that there are hardly any places in Mumbai which serve pure Maharashtrian food. Almost 90, if not 95 per cent of the restaurants serve Punjabi or Mughlai food. You will find Kerala, Bengali, Gujarati, Rajasthani restaurants in Mumbai and with the rising popularity of fish, some Konkani or Goan cuisine too but pure vegetarian Maharashtrian food is a rarity. I keep wondering if this is what we Bombayites vie for as cosmopolitanism.

Everything else, including the wedding dress, the extremely expensive clothes that the rich wear, the so-called designer clothes, indeed owes much to the ubiquitous influence of films. Perhaps you are aware that since acting wasn't supposed to an honorable profession in the 1930's till as late as the 1970's or 80's, so-called cultured and aristocratic families would not dream of allowing their daughters or daughters-in-law to act in films. The vacuum was filled in the early days by Anglo-Indian women, and a little later, Muslim women took over from them. It's hard to believe this considering that there is now a 180 degree change in the status of actresses and actors. Film stars, models and cricketers are the only celebrities today. They get elected to parliament or are nominated to the Rajya Sabha. The cynicism of the political parties may be egregious but understandable. All they want is to get more seats in parliament. Intellectuals, scholars or scientists, philosophers, sociologists, educators, thinkers, writers, activists or people who are working for the amelioration of the poor and the country no longer count. What is confounding is that the populace, the common man and woman must surely believe that these celluloid idols understand their plight and problems, they represent their interests and will fight for them. That they might be clueless doesn't seem to matter. What is clear is that Bollywood cinema has now become the most central aspect of our lives.

RLC: Why have none of your novels been adapted to film? For me reading your novels is a process that develops at multiple levels at once, and one such level is the moving image where the great epic of *God's Little Soldier*, or of *Cuckold*, a self-reflective Indian film like *Ravan and Eddie, The Extras*, or a film like *Seven Sixes are Forty Three*—all unfold in my mind with their full cinematic potential. The fragments of lives, the dynamics of human interrelationships from *Seven Sixes*... are symptomatic of the social anxiety, search for identity and confusion that Indian men and women are caught in. This could result into a truly postmodern film. What do you think keeps filmmakers from trying to create visual adaptations of your works? Your novels are highly cinematic, and as I was reading all your novels I visualized them, I *saw* them in plural forms with my mind's eye.

KN: Yes.... Well, I'm very lucky to have you as a reader. Let me first say that in the reviews of *The Extras*, only one woman has pointed out that it is like all my other work an extremely cinematic novel. At the same time, let me talk a bit about *Cuckold* and *Ravan and Eddie*. For *Cuckold* I have had at least twenty offers in the last fifteen years, and for *Ravan and Eddie* I had signed a contract in 1995 but nothing ultimately came of it. The long and the short of it is that though there have been suitors for all my novels, some of them the most famous personalities in Indian films, no book of mine has been made into a movie. *Cuckold* is a complex subject since it's such an introspective and philosophical novel while simultaneously having the potential for spectacular action and a costume drama but that too hasn't seen the light of day so far.

RLC: I believe in the quality of your writing and I know that you will manage to seduce 'lady luck' in regard to having filmic adaptations of your fiction....

KN: It intrigues me that all Marathi critics can talk about when they read *Seven Sixes are Forty-three* is alienation and the pessimism in the book, but they rarely, if ever find any humor in it or talk about the mad energy in the book, or the protagonist's greed for living every moment to the full.

RLC: Oh, but humor is a chief ingredient in *Seven Sixes are Forty Three*, and in fact in all your books, and my research work engages with all aspects of your books.

KN: I know, but that is not noticed much. Another important point about *Seven Sixes* is that it is tri-lingual as Indians often tend to be. The reason it is such a departure from mainstream Marathi literature is its highly unorthodox use of the language. As some critics have pointed out, it's as if the language is being reinvented.

RLC: You received the Sahitya Akademi Award for your novel *Cuckold* (1997), where the Maharaj Kumar is the main protagonist. Barring your book, his own claim to fame is that he was married to perhaps the most famous lover of Krishna, Mira. Often the reader gets to sympathize with Maharaj Kumar and one might say that the novel is extremely daring in its revelation of emotional and physical needs that human beings experience. You have rendered the Maharaj Kumar as an epitome of patience towards his wife Meera, and you've equally shown his strengths and weaknesses. How much of the Maharaj Kumar exists in today's Indian man? Because you have created the Maharaj Kumar, you have dealt with his psyche, and language, so I want to know how you connect the real life contemporary Indian man to the character. I think here both about a broad view, and about some particulars, the many instances of harassment that Indian women face in contemporary India.

KN: At the beginning of the novel, for the first 200 pages at least, the Maharaj Kumar is extremely upset with his wife since she has told him on their wedding night that she's betrothed to someone else and ill-treats her. I would like to digress a bit now. When I was in America as a Fulbright Associate Professor in Ithaca College, I was 'forced' at the last minute to teach my own novels. This came as a surprise to me because I had been informed that my job would be to participate in the production of my controversial play, *Bed-time Story*. Add to that I don't read my work once the books are published. Anyhow I had no option but to teach my own books. I have no idea if my students learnt anything from me but I can tell you they certainly taught me some major lessons. I had eighteen women and two boys in the class.

RLC: That is generally the case in the humanities.

KN: Yes. But I learnt with something of a shock that the women-students felt no sympathy at all for the Maharaj Kumar. Quite the contrary, he was a problem character and at fault since he had been so nasty to his wife and kicked the tumbler in which she had fetched water for him.

When I started writing the book, I did not have any clue as to where I was going. The only thing that I was sure about before I wrote the very first line of *Cuckold* was that at some point or the other the Maharaj Kumar would paint himself blue. Other than that I was improvising from moment to moment. But of course as you would know, both the unconscious and the subconscious must have been at work right through. For instance, the fact that I chose to write in contemporary English was an important decision which I must have taken even as I started to write. That decision certainly had a history. I had read Boswell's *Life of Dr. Johnson* when I was doing my second year in college. Dr. Johnson and some of the great thinkers, writers, politicians, playwrights, actors and cartoonists of that time, Sheridan, Goldsmith, Garrick, Burke, Hogarth would sit down and talk in coffee houses for hours. After all, it was the golden age of conversation but only later did it occur to me that they did not talk to each other in ancient English but in 18th century English which was quintessentially contemporary for them.

In Maharashtra, one of our great poets and mystic saints called Dnyaneshwar decided he had finished his life's work by the age of twenty-two and then the legend says he took a *samadhi;* not a normal *samadhi* but he got people to build very tight brick walls around him on all sides and bid goodbye to the world. As you are well aware when you take *samadhi*, you are not supposed to die in the normal sense of the word. But that again is an aside. But when he was alive and writing his commentary on the *Bhagwat Gita* or composing exceptionally fine sensual poetry along with intense philosophical verse, he, his brothers, sister and friends, some of them major saints themselves, all used to sit around and chat and crack jokes, laugh or discuss complex philosophical matters. How absurd it would be if we thought they used to converse in an archaic version of Marathi. So when the Maharaj Kumar lived he was speaking a contemporary Mewari, not an archaic language. If I had chosen to write *Cuckold* in Mewari, that wouldn't have done either because the Maharaj Kumar spoke 16th century Mewari. Think about it, what would have happened if I had learnt 16th century Mewari and written my novel in that ancient tongue. Naturally barring a few scholars nobody would have read it and even if they did, it would have been Greek and Latin to them.

But to get back to the earlier point, for the Maharaj Kumar it must have come as a shock that his wife would not sleep with him and that too because she was carrying on with somebody else. Let's not forget that the Maharaj Kumar came from a royal family and to watch his wife sing and dance in public was nothing less than anathema. Little wonder then that he was so upset. But the women students in my class did not see it that way. When I finally took courage in my hands and asked them how they would react if on their wedding night they discovered that their husband was sleeping with somebody else, their answer was, he would never do that. And anyway, they would have done their homework and checked every detail of his life.

I am not sure what I was to make of that answer. But later on when I spoke to the head of the department of English, he had an interesting insight. He said in the last few decades a feminist point of view completely dominated women to the exclusion of any willingness to understand what men are confronted with and the quandaries they may find themselves in. They were unable to even theoretically enter into a different time frame when the cultural and gender mores were unlike theirs. And even worse they were unable to view matters from a different point of view.

RLC: In any case, it's true the Maharaj Kumar has had some violent reactions towards his wife in various moments, but by the middle of the novel he has evolved to a point where he finds himself not only drawn to her but nurses her and cleans her up when she gets cholera and saves her life. He has indeed risen above his 'masculine ego'. As a matter of fact he has evolved so much that he becomes a different person. His impersonation of Krishna and the *gopis* shows the extremes to which he was willing to go for his wife as he develops feelings of love and affection for her.

KN: Definitely…. At the end he even admits openly that she is the only one for him. As you rightly mentioned, he evolves a lot and significantly, in the process of evolution you see him as an extremely divided human being—for instance if you think of the Bhootani Mata sequences.

RLC: Yes, that sequence is vital; it is as if he is facing his own unconscious when he meets Bhootani Mata in her cave.

KN: Yes, but something else must be emphasized. In *Cuckold*, Bhootani Mata asks the Maharaj Kumar: 'How far are you willing to go?' And he says—'Absolutely to the limit'; yet, she is able to catch him out on that, because despite his bravado statement, he is ambivalent and not sure how he wants to deal with his wife. He wants his wife Mira to be dead, but at the same time he cannot bear the thought of her being dead. He gradually goes from total hurt and wanting to do away with her, to the point where, when she gets cholera he is unable to sleep until he comes to her rescue. The Maharaj Kumar, not only nurses her round the clock, he cleans her up as the cholera becomes worse. In many ways, the Maharaj Kumar's ego is very different from that of the standard issue Rajputs who would never be doing things best left to the untouchable or Dalits as they are called now.

RLC: In fact that is what made his own people turn against him; that is why he was also called 'a cuckold', because of what they considered his 'cowardly' and 'unmanly' attitudes, because he was different from others even when he was forcing himself to fit the behavioral pattern that his society expected of him. But almost at every stage Maharaj Kumar breaks the mould of the stereotype of the Rajput prince.

KN: Right, that is why he can think of retreating as an essential part of war strategy and that is why he has commissioned a study of the subject; that is why he is willing to fight guerilla warfare; that is why he tries to avoid any battle or war if the outcome is uncertain or the victory does not secure any concrete gains in terms of territory or political advantage. His father has told him that he is a man 'before his time'. But Maharaj Kumar is also way ahead of his times because he's deeply interested in town-planning and water and sewage systems. Unlike his brother Vikramaditya he is not into sadism and while he certainly wants the crown since he is the heir apparent, he will not indulge in murder and assassination as was the wont of princes in those days. Perhaps it would have been far more beneficial to the kingdom and the subjects if he had bumped off his unscrupulous brother but he will not take that route.

To come to contemporary India, his 'time' has still not yet come, because unfortunately in so many cases Indians behave in the most questionable manner possible. Take the matter of sewage or water supply, the amelioration of his people or of public ethics, subjects that exercised the mind of the Maharaj Kumar. Or a measured, thoughtful notion of how to exercise power and negotiate with the enemy. If you recall the case of the two Indian soldiers killed by Pakistanis, and the view of some Indian politicians was that we should kill ten Pakistanis for each of our dead men.... I don't think that the Maharaj Kumar would ever support this kind of talk. However, in the same context, I must point out that there are two types of Krishna as we know today—a strange fact which is also related to the Indian character: there is the *Bhagwat Gita* Krishna, and the God who's always carrying on with women.

RLC: The philosopher and the lover....

KN: Yes, but what rules the roost today is the lover Krishna and his 16,000 *gopis* and aficionados, including the Radha figure from the *Geet-Govind*. On the other hand the philosophical *Gita* circuit which is a heavy money-earner in terms of public lectures, is a facile commentary that does not deal with the problematic nature of the *Gita* but picks the abstractions that are certainly important but rarely convey the complexity of the text to the listeners, while for the Maharaj Kumar the *Gita* philosophy is nothing less than a code of conduct for a *kshatriya* and of lived life itself. Since he had taken Krishna as his guru, in a sense he was taught the Gita by none other than the god himself. And as you know, the *Gita* offers a clear concept of dharma and responsibility whichever profession you belong to: a priest, warrior, a trader, or a workman. The Maharaj Kumar has imbibed the teachings of Krishna and assimilated them to the point where it has become the touchstone of his every action. And herein lays the cause of the tragic irony of his quandary. It is none other than that his guru and god has betrayed him and seduced his wife.

And what according to Krishna is the dharma of the *kshatriya* or warrior? It is to fulfill your destiny in the sphere your birth has chosen for you. It is only when you exert yourself to the limit to reach the full potential of your caste and its responsibilities (I like to view it also as 'vocation'), that your life becomes worthwhile. Gandhi who also found his guru in the *Gita* interprets it in his own contrary way. He makes non-violence his creed. Krishna is one of our very few gods who is Machiavellian. He's hardly ever an agent of violence. He gets somebody else to help him or commit the deed. The Maharaj Kumar has learnt his lesson well from his guru. He goes against the Kshatriya grain, because he is not one who rejoices in battle and war. He's not a warrior looking to sacrifice as many soldiers as he can but he tries to save as many of his soldiers as possible. If one is to relate the man to contemporary India, he is very much a secular person, because so long as Muslims live in his own kingdom he treats them exactly as he treats Hindus. That is why he commissions one of his Muslim assistants to write the book on retreats. As you pointed out, I think he is someone who is capable of deep thinking, and living according to the principles that he thinks are right. For me, one of the most important moments in the novel is when the Maharaj Kumar talks to Bruhannada, the eunuch. Bruhannada is the name Arjun takes in the year when he, his brothers and their common wife Draupadi were forced to live incognito for a year according to the conditions of their exile. Arjun assumes the role of Bruhannada, the eunuch in the *Mahabharata*. The pre-condition of the exile was that if anyone happened to recognize either Arjun-Bruhannada or any of the other Pandavas or Draupadi during that one year, then the fourteen-year period of exile would be repeated.

In *Cuckold,* the eunuch, Bruhannada is Queen Karmavati's advisor and the novel's éminence-grise. He quotes one of the most revered characters of the *Mahabharata*, Bhishma. Bhishma is supposed to be the epitome of everything that is ethical and the quintessence of righteousness. In a sense he is at least as much a representative of righteousness as the god Rama is. But the Maharaj Kumar points out something that Hindus would rather not confront: that Bhishma owes his loyalty to the Kauravas, the hundred cousins of the Pandavas, and *not* to a system of ethical values. So when Draupadi is disrobed, he does not raise his voice and object to the scandalous behavior of the Kauravas. It is at the point when Bruhannada is nearly killed by Queen Karmavati's son, Vikramaditya that the Maharaj Kumar asks Bruhannada what he thinks is more valuable: loyalty to a set of people or to a set of ethical values? It is a question which makes the eunuch rethink his life and choices and the Maharaj Kumar is able to change Bruhannada's mind. Unfortunately, Bruhannada is killed before he gives his damning testimony to the court of law. Throughout the book, Maharaj Kumar's thinking goes against the accepted wisdom of Indians and he does things which many Indians find difficult to accept and moreover, to follow.

RLC: I think one essential point in the distinction or comparison between Maharaj Kumar and the contemporary man is the capacity to take responsibility for one's own acts and decisions.

NK: That's an acute observation. Let me add an aside here. The science of retreat is something that most Indians today would not want to understand and accept at all. Since the time the Chinese attacked us in 1962, we've been behaving in an acutely myopic fashion. We don't understand the importance of the notion of retreat, which the Maharaj Kumar's father did not understand either. When the Mewar armies are defeated by Babur, it is the Maharaj Kumar who tells his father—"So what? What we have going for us is a long memory and a capacity to wait till the time is right and ripe. We'll modernize our armed forces and our weaponry and with time, patience and a calculated strategy we will be prepared far better for the next encounter."

RLC: But the way the Maharaj Kumar is killed, by betrayal, is in fact a response to the fact that the society is not ready for people like him. What is your take on the way he dies in the novel?

KN: Let me first say that I did not really know how to end the novel till everything fell in place at the last minute. There is a story, a myth, that it was Mira who disappeared into the marble idol of Shri Krishna. I transferred the whole event to the Maharaj Kumar because, as Krishna says, there is no division or dichotomy between him and the Prince. The Maharaj Kumar may have begun to hate Krishna but in the end Krishna has the last word. He is such a shrewd, smart and sly god, he always manages to have his way.

RLC: Indeed, he is an exquisitely duplicitous god.... Still, my stress is on the fact that you made a *man*, Maharaj Kumar, and not a woman disappear into (or merge with) a male deity idol. Why is that?

KN: Probably because Krishna can never find a disciple who is as deeply into the Krishna philosophy as the Maharaj Kumar is. More important is the fact that people are bundles of contradictions, which is evident in the Maharaj Kumar. Besides let's not forget the act of enveloping the Prince within himself is initiated by Shri Krishna.

RLC: Now I will ask something meant to take us gradually towards the intertextuality found in your work. Who are the Indian and Western authors who have influenced your writing in terms of character portrayal, approach, or style and criticism and why did they influence you?

KN: I must confess that there are many authors who have had a strong impact on me and I am truly grateful to them for creating such classics. But I think their influence was subterranean because my writing is very different from the authors that I think the world of. For instance,

Graham Greene—I think he is a superb writer. The French author Céline who was unfortunately extremely anti-Semitic, and yet despite this awful prejudice, it is difficult to understand 20th century literature without Céline's writing and the enormous influence it had—the black humor, the velocity of writing, the stop-go writing, the humor in it. It is absolutely astounding and we hardly ever talk about it. Then there is Camus, whose compassion I absolutely treasure. How can I forget the old-time greats like Tolstoy, Dostoyevsky.... I like the American writer James Leo Herlihy who wrote *Midnight Cowboy*, which was made into a film with Dustin Hoffman and Jon Voight, I love Joseph Heller and his *Catch-22*, but I do not find their overt influence in my writing, maybe the readers would be able to spot it. It's not at all that I deny any influence. I remember Coleridge had stated that you have to be a stone not to be influenced, but at some point in time you have to find your own voice.

RLC: Your texts are rich in intertextual references which would make the reader take each thread, go and discover those interlinks, meanings and their significance in your novels. For instance, after finding so many references to *Dirty Harry*, I watched the film, then I re-read the passages pointing to different sequences and moments of the film and my visual of your novel acquired other levels of meaning. Of course, this is essential in the comparative research process, but any readers for that matter, if they get engaged with the subtexts and intertexts, expand their reading experience and encounter an even richer novel. I don't say that without intertextual reference a novel cannot be rich, but intertextuality adds information and complexity to the subject and meanings.

KN: You are right, and in the last two decades there has been a serious movement towards quotation, especially in cinema, not only in fiction. I have internalized so much of other authors and that is bound to out one way or another. But I do not limit myself to quoting others, I want to tell my story. There are hundreds of occasions where I have used references from other texts like the *Iliad*, *Mahabharata* etc. For instance, in *The Extras* I use Sita and Ravan, but in a contrary fashion. Ravan is the arch enemy of Rama, the most righteous of gods and it is the mythological Ravan who has kidnapped Rama's wife, Sita in *The Extras*. But in *The Extras* it's the bride, Sita who falls for Ravan and takes him to bed on her wedding night. The curious thing is that I didn't set out to create these strange resonances.

RLC: That is one peculiarity of your novels; one cannot simply place one novel in a particular category and define it—'this novel is this or that', one cannot simply categorize your work and say it resembles another novel or fiction. Your style has its intricacy and it changes from novel to novel, your language quirks and wit make humor melt into tragedy, romance into comedy, individual drama into history, and so on.

KN: I fervently hope all my novels are different from each other. As said the subject dictates the style for me, and that is how my books perhaps are so different from each other, since the subjects bear no similarity amongst themselves. But whether they do or not, is for the reader and critic to judge. After having read my essay *Shiva's Blue Throat*, you know that, while I think that Rushdie is a hell of an author, somehow after a point I cannot take his writing because he goes on repeating himself.

RLC: I agree, exactly as you argue in *Shiva's Blue Throat* about a writer's connection with the text—when the author writes he takes in the poison which gets absorbed in the body. Of course it's metaphoric poison, but similarly the reader takes in what s/he reads and processes the intake until the end or up to a point where the reader feels resistance to further reading the full text and may stop midway.... With some authors, 'the style is the man'....

KN: 'The style is the man' does not work for me, that is why I let the subject lead me to the style in each case, in each novel.... Anyway, among contemporary Indian authors I appreciate Amitav Ghosh and especially his text *Shadow Lines*, because in his other books, for instance *The Hungry Tide*, research overwhelms the fiction. It is admirable how much research he has done, but it is often not internalized and assimilated into his fiction.

RLC: Yes, Amitav Ghosh deals with serious historical research, so his writing may serve as very good texts for studies in Indian history and society.

KN: I cannot underestimate the role the mystic saints of India have played in formulating, I dare not call it my philosophy, but my mindset and what I value in life. Overall, I hope that the new generation of Indian writers will imbibe rigour, robustness, and a passion for life and integrity from our mystic-poets and bring a new vigour to the writing in the subcontinent.

RLC: Regarding the mystics and saints, your character of Shakta Muni from *God's Little Soldier* was an intriguing product—a guru, a businessman, an armaments dealer.... Why? Is the creation of this character a criticism to many fake gurus who populate India and the world?

KN: Of course, there are innumerable bogus gurus in India. But the fact is many politicians, including Indira Gandhi and Narasimha Rao had Tantric gurus, and they were both involved in the armaments business, including connections with the well-known armament dealer Adnan Khashoggi. So the fictional Shakta Muni character borrows a lot from reality and the lived life of India. I think of Shakta Muni as an amazing ominous éminence-grise, but it's also commonly bruited that there are some Tantric gurus who are said to have amazing powers and skills.

RLC: Have you researched the Tantric practices and effects on the human self? I think about Zia's experiences and hallucinations for instance and his change of identity into Tejas etc.

KN: Yes, I have done a bit of research on this, but I didn't live in any ashram in the company of tantric gurus. I was extremely lucky to be given permission to stay in a Trappist monastery. As I have said earlier, for me research is important but only as hand maiden to the writing of fiction and it is the imagination and the capacity to live other lives through the imagination which are of primary importance in the creative arts. It was very difficult to find a monastery which would accept me, especially since I happened to be a Hindu, but a stern, and yet kind-at-heart and generous Abbot allowed me to stay in a monastery for a few months. I don't think the book would have been possible without him because I lived and worked there. In fact both the Abbot and Zia's father, Abbajaan are the most generous and compassionate characters in my book. Zia's father is a fine human being and he sees Zia for what he is; he even portrays him as 'Judas' in a sculpture he creates for the new church he designs.

RLC: These interreligious comparisons appear at various moments through the book. Amanat too evokes different kinds of imagery in his story *The Arsonist*—a novel-within-the-novel—and in the building he designs for Zia or rather Lucens's new philanthropic venture.

KN: I am happy that Amanat did not turn out to be a one-dimensional character or a mere counterpoint to Zia. In his letters to his brother, Amanat often raises crucial questions about several subjects and comments on them directly or obliquely. For instance, he attempts to understand how a believer of the Holy Book can explain Hitler, Stalin, Idi Amin and other such monsters in a world purported to be created by the all merciful-and-compassionate Almighty.

RLC: Amanat has those dreams and visions about corpses, putrid bodies, and words eating human flesh. I interpret them as metaphors for human violence, the evil that exists in any society, the destruction of the world, war, symptoms of decaying souls and bodies, especially because Amanat has had serious health problems. How did you come to include such surreal, horrendous images?

KN: I would like to refer again to *Shiva's Blue Throat*. I prefer to let the readers interpret the metaphors through the multiple levels of meanings. I think one of the early letters of Amanat is about words; later he talks about allergies and his asthma. Apart from the fact that the letters are also satirical, Amanat is genuine in his attempt to deal with reality. At some point there is a reference to Swift's famous essay "A Modest Proposal", where there is the imagery of people eating babies during the Irish famine. Man's violence towards man is beyond comprehension. Gandhiji had a simple but incontrovertible insight about this, 'An eye for an eye will live the world blind.'

RLC: The trouble is that many self-confessed 'Gandhians' loudly mention this quote and many others in their 'speech' at various points, while the next moment they make offensive statements dredging deep into our subconscious and tapping into our deepest prejudices about other communities or countries which subliminally instigate people to hatred and violence. We have heard such statements as 'Muslims are bad', 'Westerners are racist' and so on. Of course in all communities, there are people who see things, who consider people and the world in racial (or racist) terms—they can be conservative Christians, Muslims, Hindus etc. Especially if religion is the main criterion of division, the conflicts are more challenging. That is why I always emphasize the distinction between 'spirituality' and 'religion' which many people confuse.

KN: Yes, you are so right about this. I wanted to draw your attention to another letter where Amanat describes a painting he sees in the Detroit Museum of Art. That is an imaginary painting which has a bracket at the bottom—which is a common practice after the name of artist. There is a name, then the year of birth, a hyphen and a space, because the artist is alive and there's no closure yet. That becomes the open mouth of fate perpetually waiting to swallow each one of us up.

RLC: Why haven't you published your play *Bedtime Story*?

KN: Well, initially because of a censorship controversy I could not find any publisher. The play ultimately had twenty-five performances in Marathi and four in Hindi. The actors enjoyed acting in the play so much they spent their own money on translating it into Hindi, then performed it.

RLC: What made you write the play at that point in time, in the 1970s? What is the philosophy behind it?

KN: I think the play was primarily written as a criticism of myself. In those times we did not get too much news from abroad, and the only magazines I got to read occasionally were office copies of *Time* and *Newsweek*. Thanks to their slanted reportage I was oblivious of the fact that Ho Chi Minh was elected through a democratic election, whereas the American media tried to make out that his election was illegal and the results were engineered by Ho Chi Minh. So when I also read a biography of Ho Chi Minh and another of Fidel Castro, I came to know about their lives and what they were fighting for. Soon after starting to write the play, Mrs. Indira Gandhi declared the Emergency which made the play far more urgent and far more relevant; since initially our response to the dismissal of the Parliament in Mumbai was lukewarm. The one exception from the very start was Ramnath Goenka's powerful resistance to it through his newspaper *The Indian Express*. But over a period of time the protests grew louder different opposition leaders were sent to prison and Mrs Gandhi's son, Sanjay Gandhi managed to enrage vast numbers of people because of forced sterilizations and other actions. Simultaneously there was no denying the growing international criticism. Mrs Gandhi then made the mistake of calling an election. She lost badly and it looked as if her career was over.

What happened to the country at this juncture is crucial. It is a fact that people rarely get a second chance at life, but when our polity actually was lucky enough to get this rarest gift of a second chance, it was terrible to watch the politicians who had cobbled a new party from the various factions destroy the new mandate by squabbling endlessly amongst themselves.

RLC: I think a major problem is that India is still not ready to face its realities, which may be the case with others too. Many problems are carried unresolved from one age to another, from one generation to another. And your play is still so relevant for contemporary India, because it reveals several realities which many people do not want to admit; I speak about the inter-human relations, the individuals and the society at large. I feel that the Indian psyche still struggles and avoids accepting or facing its problems, and this affects both people and culture or more precisely, the 'cultural self'. What is your opinion about this? Because in any situations of conflict, harassment and other circumstances, those who are less powerful, or in minority, are generally blamed and put in the line of attack.

KN: I think you are right. But *Bed-time Story* applies as much to India as to the entire world. From a longer perspective one can see that people suffer from extreme short-sightedness. When you think about the regional parties and their persecution of minorities, the rapes of women, and the way some politicians including women, handle such problems, one can only gasp at their total lack of a sense of justice while their insensitivity to the plight of others is staggering. My play says a lot about these situations too. Its central thrust is indifference, apathy and all the sins that issue forth from the crime which goes by the name 'What can I do?' *Bed-time* Story's theme is more relevant at this particular point in time than ever before for the reason that fossil fuels and rampant consumption have damaged the ecological equilibrium to the point where thousands of species have disappeared and humankind itself is faced with extinction in many parts of the world. Unfortunately the play itself has not been published yet.

RLC: A significant point you make occurs in the first act of the play which deals with caste problems in the guise of Eklavya.

KN: I have known the story of Eklavya from the *Mahabharata* since childhood. It is told to every child with a great deal of reverence as a paradigm of the *guru-shishya parampara* or the teacher-pupil tradition. Eklavya, the tribal prince out-classes Arjun, one of the five Pandava brothers, who is supposed to be the finest archer in the world. But, Dronacharya, the guru of both the Pandavas as well as their cousins, the hundred Kauravas, firmly puts Eklavya in his place by asking the tribal prince for his right thumb. We are all supposed to follow Eklavya's example as the ideal pupil who will make any sacrifice for his teacher. It was only when I began to write the play that I understood the enormous injustice of what the teacher demands and came up with a befitting answer from the pupil who has understood the dynamics of the situation perfectly.

But the Dalit issue raises many other questions, one of the most important being how the political parties in power ignore them till election time when suddenly they wake up and try to buy them off with increased reserved quotas. You can't blame the Dalits for having become dependent on these hand-outs and yet it is truly tragic that nearly seventy years after Independence they prefer not to see through these crass ploys. If only they would demand a ten-fold increase in the money spent on their education so that they will get the finest teachers specially trained with the specific objective that no Dalit will ever want a handout and will compete neck to neck with the so-called higher castes, do well enough to get the best jobs and never again feel inferior to anybody.

RLC: Yes but to emphasize a point from the play, it is significant that in your play Drona himself states—"A Bhil, a Mahar, a leper. There's no place for subtle distinctions among Untouchables." This is remarkably relevant to the present times, because if someone like Drona—a teacher, a professor who is supposed to nurture and mould the character of the students—has such mind-frame, then the inquiry goes further and involves questions about the ontology of knowledge, the evolution of society. If one goes on teaching and imbedding these distinctions in the young people's minds—i.e. 'this one is untouchable', 'this is bad' etc.—then that is extremely problematic. This 'Drona paradigm' is relevant for many teachers in today's world, who circulate erroneous information and stereotypes which most students do not question and accept as such.

KN: The finer distinctions you make are indeed valid. And yes when we look at the world we find many such problems everywhere.

RLC: Thank you so much for your time and your thoughtful responses to my queries.

KN: Thank you for your patience.

❑❑❑

Post-Perestroika Challenges in Russian Political Drama

VERA SHAMINA

IN Russia theatre has always been highly politicized and performed different functions at different times: it was a means of emancipation of the internal energy of the masses during the first years following the 1917 October revolution, a mouthpiece of ideological dictatorship during the period of Stalin's rule, a voice of forbidden truth in the years of "stagnation"[1] and eventually a school for democracy, teaching people to think and speak freely thus preparing the acquisition of internal freedom. However, it was absolutely impossible to expose any current policy or directly show any living political figures in a play and the genre of political drama as such appeared actually only after perestroika with the emergence of the so-called Russian "new drama" in the 1990s. In order to understand why and how it happened that the genre so productive in the West only recently came into being in Russia we should turn back to history.

Historical Flashback

It was as early as in the 1930s when a certain procedure of state quality control for all theatres was established. If a play was new it was strictly revised by the censors before it could appear on stage. After all the "corrections" and cuts were made the show was presented for acceptance to a special commission comprising the members of local party authorities and Ministry of Culture. The "high" judges tried hard to find disloyalty, allegory, and dangerous double meaning. Directors had to fight for each production, changing accents, trying to satisfy the tastes of the party authorities. Paradoxical as it may seem censorship at the same time played a positive role in the development of theatrical mastery. Theatres acquired refinement in the art of allusions, hints and implications, and the spectators—in decoding them. It looked as if there was a constant competition between the performers, spectators and the censors—who would be the most quick-witted. The aesthetics of implications stirred the mind, and the spectators actually became coauthors of such productions, adding the meaning, which could not be articulated. In such a way theatres often addressed current political issues using Aesopian language.

In the 1970s this type of theatre was supplemented by the so-called "production drama". While the government policy was still a taboo, at least it became possible to speak about economic concerns. The success of these dramas with the public could be explained by the fact that at this time the country was led into an economic deadlock, and theatres became the place, where these issues could be discussed. The protagonist of these plays was a young energetic and enterprising young man, who did not want to live as of old, rejected the undeserved bonuses, told the truth to his employers, and struggled with the bureaucracy. The titles of these plays are telling by themselves: *A Person from the Outside, Bonus; We, the Undersigned; The Minutes of One Meeting.* Each of these performances turned into a production meeting where most burning economic problems were raised. To some extent these shows made up for the deficit of truth in the country. However very soon it became evident that production drama did not justify the hopes pinned on it. Due to the objective insolubility of the production conflict the conflict of the play itself was either removed or remained open.

At the beginning of the 1980s after Leonid Brezhnev's death, when Communist Party leaders exchanged each other at the helm of power being more concerned about personal health than about the state of affairs in the country there was a considerable relief of censorship in the theatre. One of its remarkable results was the appearance of historic dramas featuring the events of the 1917 October revolution and first years of Soviet rule. It was an attempt to destroy ideological stereotypes and give a new interpretation of the Soviet history, as for a long time many historical documents referring to this time were kept in closed archives. A key figure in this process was Mikhail Shatrov. He wrote many plays about Vladimir Lenin and the Bolsheviks and was actually the first to introduce political drama based on historical material. The peak of his popularity was in the second half of the 1980s—the time of perestroika, when it became possible to talk about the Bolshevik leaders as common people with their strong and weak points, doubts they had and mistakes they made. And since perestroika was actually another revolution all subjects connected with the October revolution 1917 aroused great interest.

Shatrov's plays became the source of elementary knowledge for many people of the history of their country. This interest was increased by the fact that the characters of these plays were historic figures, which for a long time had been deleted from Soviet historiography. Besides, these plays appealed to the public by their unorthodox treatment of historic facts, the moral, psychological and philosophical problems they raised and helped to promote political thinking as many of the issues he addressed, mainly those of the people and the power, were very topical for the time of radical political changes in society. All these features were especially brightly reflected in the production of Shatrov's play *Dictatorship of Conscience* (1986). The play was conceived as a public debate. The author brings back the tradition of the revolutionary *agit-trials,*[2] in such a way the playwright invites the audience to revise the past from a modern standpoint. The split in Russian society of the 1980s, the appearance of different viewpoints on the fate and the very essence of socialist ideas inspired the playwright to stage a trial of Lenin. The authorial text in this play is intersected with quotations from documents, letters and fiction; the play features historical personalities together with fictional characters, who embody the ideas discussed in the play. All of them speak at the improvised trial of Lenin, giving their evidence. Mikhail Shatrov raised the problems which concerned not just the understanding of the past but were also topical for the present and future of the country: what is an individual—a cog in the state machine or the final goal and meaning of a revolutionary struggle? What is his/her place in history? The theatre of perestroika appealed to the audience directly voicing the early forbidden truth and involving the spectators into an active reassessment of their past and emancipating from it.[3]

During the first years of perestroika, the main bulk of plays run at the theatres mostly comprised those written as they said "into the drawer", that is written in the period of "stagnation" but unpublished for censorship reasons. They were enthusiastically hailed by audiences as the first words of truth. The record-breaker among them was a satirical comedy by Mikhail Roshchin, *The Seventh Labor of Heracles*, written as many others long before—in 1966 and staged only in 1989. This play summarized the era of "stagnation". The play is based on the myth of Augean stables cleaned by Heracles. In the playwright's interpretation it became a direct analogy of what had been going on for a long time in Russia. The action unfolds itself in Elis, whose greatest pride is Augean stables. The whole country stinks with manure but all its inhabitants claim that it is the smell of sandalwood and roses. Lie assumed here the aspect of Truth; Aite, the goddess of delusion accompanies the inhabitants of Elis throughout their whole life: she makes speeches, answers questions and speaks words of love for them. But what is worse, the majority of the people have got so accustomed to this situation that they don't notice it. And one day the monument to Heracles comes to life and is shocked by what he sees. The old road-sweeper tells him: "While you were sleeping they punished and pardoned on your behalf!" Moreover, when Heracles offers to Augeas to clean his stables, the latter refuses as he is afraid that the whole world will learn that the stables have not been cleaned for thirty years, and the stink of exposure may poison the souls of the citizens. Even the most unsophisticated audience member did not fail to recognize in such a declaration the considerations of the authorities, their fear of publicity and their conviction that if the appearances are saved people can feel happy and contented. At the same time, Roshchin's play set one of the key topics of perestroika—the discrepancy between the festive facade and the boondocks of real life with their poverty, squalor and crippled fates of people.

The repertory of the first perestroika years demonstrated that for many playwrights the years of stagnation were not futile—they wrote the truth which had been waiting for its hour to come, tried to clean the "Augean stables" or at least claim that the country was drowning in filth. The plays of Liudmila Petrushevskaia, Alexei Dudarev, Liudmila Razumovskaia, Alexander Galin, Victor Slavkin, Nikolai Koliada and some other playwrights written on formerly forbidden themes can be called "political" even though they did not feature any political events as such. They were the acts of civil righteousness and audiences hailed their antifestive, antiofficial character. Still everyone expected that after the verdict on the past and exposure of the ills of the present there would appear new plays marking a new stage of development in Russian theater.

The turbulence of the 1980s with their heated political debates was surpassed by the economic and political crisis of the 1990s, when the euphoria generated by the believes and hopes for the renovation of the public life and establishment of social justice gave way to disappointment and understanding that people once again were cheated and deceived by the powers that be. Besides, the 1990s were marked by the development of a postmodern situation, which brought about new mentality, new sets of values. On the one hand, the mass consciousness so deeply rooted in Russia during the years of the Soviet rule gave way to an individual consciousness of the "private person", which gained value irrespective of his/her political views and social position. The theater and literature started to focus on marginal heroes with their personal outlook and attitude to the world. At the same time according to many critics it was during this period that the crisis in Russian theatre reached its peak.[4] What used to be innovative became a cliché: demonstration of violence, promiscuity, obscene gestures and language—all this had become indispensable attributes of each play. The notion of "naked truth" started to be taken literary—and it was very seldom that a show would do without naked people or sexual intercourse on stage, no matter if it was required or not by the plot. While the audiences of the 1960-1980s learnt to read "between the lines" and the theaters excelled in allegories developing sophisticated metaphoric language, in the 1990s its place was taken by flat naturalism. Whereas the former ideological theatre substituted moral values with a simplified ideological scheme, modern theatre developed a number of steadfast clichés cashing in on sore subjects which became an obvious attempt to follow the fashion, timeserving attributes of commercial success. However it was during this period that Russian "new drama" came into being introducing some really talented and prolific authors, such as Oleg Bogaiev, Mikhail Ugarov, Iurii Klavdiiev, Ivan Viripaiev, Evgeni Grishkovets, Olga Mukhina, Maksim Kurochkin, the Presniakov brothers and some others. Still the majority rather repeated what had been done before than created anything radically new. What is more, as Birgit Beumers and Mark Lipovetsky justly point out, "… ND (new drama) completely lacks the moral pathos, which was so important for the hypo naturalism of the times of perestroika. The authors of ND do not believe in the purifying power of the truth not least because this belief miserably failed exactly in the 1990s" (19).[5] It was then that a new breakthrough, connected with the experiments of documentary and political theatre, took place.

New Challenges-New Creative Urge

More than 20 years have passed since Perestroika. When it started people felt that they were holding democracy in their hands. Much has changed since then, and such words as "civic society," "freedom," and "democracy" acquired negative meaning for many people. The belief that people can change anything in the life of the country has been long lost. The disappointment in the results of Perestroika—a lack of true democracy, the hypocrisy of the authorities, their reluctance or inability to modernize the state system, the war in Chechnya, the disillusionment of the younger generation, ethnic conflicts—urged the playwrights to look for new ways and forms of addressing reality which was found in the new type of theatre based on facts and documents where fictitious characters and situations were replaced by real people articulating their problems and live political figures. And as a result, a new type of drama, directly addressing the most burning problems of the new Russia came into being. Whereas in the West, documentary theater as a genre is far from being new and played an especially important role in the XXth century, in Russia it pioneered at the beginning of the 2000s after the seminars conducted in Moscow by the directors of *Royal Court,* Stephen Daldry and James MacDonald from November 1999 till April 2000. They introduced the technique of *verbatim***,** the author's use of exact interviews in the script, to young Russian playwrights. This stimulated the appearance of new plays based on this technique and the creation of *Theatre.Doc*. in 2002, which became a testing ground for young playwrights who experimented in this genre. "In a country much maligned for its harsh restrictions of the press and free speech, this new brand of gritty, low-budget theater has been attracting attention for tackling social and sometimes political issues that nobody else will"—wrote Byron Asher in her essay "In Russia's 'New Drama,' Chekhov Is Out, Grit Is In".

In 2004, the first collection of documentary plays was published, which demonstrated the possibilities of this genre. The collection comprises 12 plays based on the interviews with Kuzbas miners, soldiers' mothers, internet users, polit-technologists, *Nord-Ost* hostages,[6] teenage fans and creators of talk shows. Life texture, the voice of the crowd, snapshots of modern Russia, the reality in which people live, but often prefer to ignore—all of this turned out to be more exciting than most bold fantasies. It became clear that this sort of drama helps to promote understanding and dialogue between people with differing points of views and get a true comprehensive picture of what occurred in a specific occasion through the process of hearing the subjective opinions of the people involved. The tour of different spheres of modern Russian reality—prisons, mines, the margins of urban markets, TV backstage, the world of political PR introduced the public to the material seldom featured by traditional theatre and made the playwrights look for new ways of expression and developing theatrical traditions.

Another experiment of *Theatre.doc* was *Witnesses' Theatre*—the authors of this project invited several detained oppositionists, sat them on stage and asked to tell the spectators how they were treated in the remand prison where they had spent two weeks. One more bold project was carried out by this theatre in 2012, based on the play by a famous Italian playwright and actor Dario Fo titled *The Two-Headed Anomaly*—in the Russian version *BerlusPutin*. The story is told on behalf of a young film director and an aging actress, who have been cast as Putin's wife Liudmila. The characters rehearse the episodes of the film, in which the surgeons transplant half of Berlusconi's brain into Putin's head. Putin is suffering from amnesia, and his wife reminds him of some episodes of his life. The show was sold out, which Tony Halpin, Moscow correspondent of *The Times,* explains by the "readiness to mock Mr. Putin and address previously taboo subjects". However it should be noted that the government tried to shut it down several months ago and although it managed to re-open, its future is very precarious.

Still, generally speaking, the last decade has been very productive in this respect: documentary plays and documentary theatres have appeared all over Russia. What is more, documentary theatre has promoted the development of Russian political drama, which being based both on real and fictive situations, using both real and fictive characters extensively incorporates factional, documentary material, bringing together art and politics. Here I would like to specify what is meant by the term "political drama". I side with Barbara Olazcec, who sticks to a broad understanding of politics in this genre, which means the exposure of the events and mode of action connected with the activity of state authority (166).

Putin.Doc

A most emblematic example of this kind of drama is a collection of plays published in 2005 under the title *Putin.doc. Nine Revolutionary Plays*. Being very different in style and form they have one distinct feature in common—all of them are highly politically committed and provide a vivid picture of the new concerns of the post-Perestroika playwrights. The plays put together in this collection are so sharp and topical that not every theatre would dare to stage them even with the absence of official censorship. Some are scandalous, some—satirically absurd, set in the past, present and even hypothetical future they make you depressed, appalled and sometimes highly amused.

Different as they are, all of them demonstrate the authors' attitude to the current authorities, the complicated situation, in which the country has found itself and relate the truth about present day Russia. Critic Pavel Rudnev calls these playwrights Russian "Angry young men", stating that new generations of playwrights usually ripen in the periods of social clashes, as it is theatre that is most capable of feeling the very "nerve of the time" reflecting the "tension of the world outlook in the marginal epochs" (6). Having read the plays enclosed, one is introduced to the most burning issues of the time and the topics Russian public is mostly concerned with. Basically there are two major groups of themes which are mostly speculated on: the relationship of the powers that be with people, involving the fate of democracy, corruption in the higher echelons, mafia controlled economy, official hypocrisy; and the war in Chechnya with the consequences it caused, such as the orgy of terrorism and intolerance in society.

The collection opens with the titular play by Victor Teterin *Putin.doc*, a satirical farce, which ridicules traditional Russian servility. The plot is quite simple: it features two fans of president Putin, quite recognizable figures—Piotr Ivanov, a high ranking officer, and Ivan Petrov, a representative of local administration, who decide to compete in their worship of the president. As the action unfolds, the situation grows more and more absurd: one changes his name to Vladimir Putin, the other—has plastic surgery and becomes Putin's double. Still it is not the limit. The friends cannot decide whose worship is stronger, so they come out to Red Square, and while one is praying to Putin's portrait, the other is masturbating in front of it. Eventually both are rewarded—they get high posts in president's administration, as according to the play the latter appreciated the subject of their competition.

The theme of the powers that be is developed by Andrei Malgin, who wrote a sequel of his satirical novel *Advisor to President* featuring the adventures of the main character in his play *Prisiadkin in the Other World*. In this play Ignatii Prisiadkin, an aging advisor and a former human rights defender (a kind of career not altogether impossible), starts losing his memory and is getting more and more confused: thus he denounces government policy speaking to foreign journalists and ardently supports it among the Kremlin authorities. His wife and his daughter are mostly concerned about losing governmental privileges. His wife takes close to heart that their status has started to decrease, it is comically shown in the scene when instead of the *BMW*, which used to take their daughter Masha to school, a *Volga* is sent: "Poor, poor Masha!"—she cries. "How will she endure such humiliation, what will happen when it becomes known at school?! Is it possible that she will come to school in a *Volga* like a daughter of some collective farm chairman?! What a disaster! Scum! Scum!" (103). Therefore when Prisiadkin finally dies, to keep the benefits his wife pretends that he is alive: she has his corpse embalmed and gives interviews instead of him. But in the long run the corpse returns to life in quite a good shape and with completely "improved" mentality: now Prisiadkin is an unconditional supporter of the ruling party and its leader, regaining his position in the corridors of power. He feels quite happy: "What do I need blood for? What do I need heart for? What do I, a government authority, need all this for? I, a member of the Russian President's Administration?!" (124). The end is symbolic. Having regained his post Prisiadkin finds out that he is not unique and all the other Administration members are zombies like him.

The comedy *Meat* by Olga Pogodina is dedicated to the state of rural economics: *Tsar* orders his *Oprichnik* to find meat produced in Russia. *Oprichnik* sends *Soldier* into a distant Siberian province, where the latter finds a family who owns a *She-goat*, which he brings to Moscow. On the way he meets *Devil* who speaks with a heavy Caucasian accent and is trying to ruin *Tsar's* plan. Eventually *She-goat* turns out to be an American spy, Jane, and *Devil* blows everyone up.

Grotesque as they are, all characters and situations in the aforementioned plays are quite recognizable and some names are just slightly changed. The president himself appears in two of the plays, and extracts of his speeches are inserted into the text. Olga Pogodina, the author of *Meat* used materials from the report of the Department of Agriculture titled *The Updated Forecast of Social and Industrial Development of the Agroindustrial Complex for 2004-2006*.

If the theme of power and government authorities is mostly treated in a farcical way with the elements of the theatre of the absurd, the other recurrent theme, the war in Chechnya and its consequences, is represented in a different key leaving little space for fun or mockery. Still such plays are also not uniform and involve different elements of theatrical conventions. The play by Piotr Filimonov *Shapito-jurt* is subtitled *Circus Parade with a Machinegun.* In it two former clown-partners who used to work together for many years in the same circus meet during the war in Chechnya. "Hi, Bim!" says the Russian, "Hi, Bom!" retorts the Chechen fighter. Thus from the very beginning the war is viewed as a bloody circus parade where both Russian and Chechen soldiers are nothing but clowns, manipulated by the "directors". The dialogue of these two people reveals the absurdity of the war, which stirs hatred among former friends and colleagues; each of them has their truth and their delusions that the war can only intensify. The allegoric figures called *Russian Understanding of War* and *Chechen Understanding of War,* which appear close to the end, do not add much to their unfinished dispute, however they help to reveal the truth about the death of the Russian soldier's daughter, who was not killed by the Chechens as he thought, but died accidentally.

The other pacifist play *Sentinel,* by Sergei Reshetnikov, portrays two friends; one who fought in Chechnya and the other, who deserted from the army being unable to endure the hazing. The latter constantly speaks to Boris Yeltsin, urging him to end the war in Chechnya and rewrite the Constitution. Mr. President answers evasively, constantly referring to the "difficulty" of the situation. As a matter of fact, the majority of playwrights who write about Chechnya have second-hand evidence taken from mass media and internet; maybe that is why so far there are no full-blooded plays of true artistic value on this subject.

Although the play *We, You, They…*by Dmitrii Istranin is not about the war as such, it is closely connected with its consequences, mainly national intolerance, which has recently become a number one problem in Russia. It shows a common school torn by the national conflict between the Chechen and Russian students referred to as "Blacks" and "Whites". In a way it continues the theme, which is one of the most recurrent in Russian new drama—the theme of juvenile violence, showing teenagers, who, having faced the cruelty of the world, respond with even surpassing brutality. The play is absolutely shocking both in its naturalistic style and in the treatment of the subject itself. The school featured by the playwright is totally controlled by the "Blacks," who taunt, humiliate and fiercely beat up the "Whites," and when the latter try to repulse the principle, the teachers and the police (as a matter of fact the one who investigates the case is also Caucasian by birth) disregarding the evidence, lay the blame completely on the Russian students and accuse them of fascism. Having failed to restore justice (they were accused of almost beating their friend to death, while it was done by the Chechens), three Russian students pour gasoline over themselves and threaten to set themselves on fire.

Unfortunately a situation like this is not absolutely impossible. Similar cases are often reported in the internet and mass media. What is really surprising, to put it mildly, is the standpoint of the author, who like his characters does not see any other solution of the problem than hatred and ruthless violence. He altogether supports his adolescent characters, who curse and menace each other using obscene language:

> **Iaroslav** (Russian). Do you want problems? School is the territory of the Whites, forgot?!
>
> **Seid** (Chechen). Wrong, bastard, wrong! Everything here is ours! Fuck you all! Roll your balls out of here or we'll kick the guts out of you.
>
> **Iaroslav**. Not afraid of law?
>
> **Lechi** (Chechen). You don't have any law, asshole, we are your law! You gonna do what we tell you or be like this one (kicks the motionless body lying on the floor). It is our time, nobody else's, put that in your pipe and smoke it.
>
> **Seid**. Our neighborhood—our school. No cop would touch us, and those Russian bastards who are still there are fed by our money, understand, motherfucker?! (130-31)

The author's message is quite transparent and explicit. The school in the play stands for the country, poisoned by social alienation, hatred and intolerance, where violence has become the norm of existence not only for the problem youth but evidently for the playwright himself, who does not allow even a slightest possibility of compassion and understanding. According to Birgit Beumers and Mark Lipovetsky, in plays like this "Communicative violence is highlighted as a "natural", commonly understood language of power and submission, which has substituted the soviet ideological doctrine and the corresponding rules of behavior. Undoubtedly such function of violence...suggests the failure or rather absence of productive attempts to build a nonviolent system of social relationships based on dialog and compromise; roughly speaking—the absence of democratic institutions and democratic policy in the post-soviet Russia" (365-66).

Here I would like to recall the project *September.doc* staged in 2005 by Mikhail Ugarov and Ruslan Malikov in the aforementioned *Theatre.doc*. It was totally based on verbatim technique and revealed the reaction of people of different nationalities to the Beslan tragedy.[7] The material was taken from Chechen, Ossetic and Russian internet forums with minimal editing; the role of the authors was mainly compilation. The aim of the authors of *September.doc.* was to give the whole specter of polar opinions on the terrorist act that shook the world. Shocking and provoking as it is, the audience hears the voices of wild chauvinists, racists, fanatic nationalists and narrow-minded philistines. The main difference of this project from the play analyzed above is that here we see both parties equally unattractive, to put it mildly, reflecting as if in a distorting mirror the monstrous social discord corroding the society and futility of mutual insults, which can only aggravate the situation.

Another way of coexistence between nations, in this case a peaceful one, is offered by Vladimir Zabaluiev and Alexei Zenzinov in their play *Smog*. The action takes place in future on a spaceship, where two astronauts—Russian and American are working together. The title refers to the situation on the Earth where everything is wrapped in smog. The spacemen converse quite peacefully until interrupted by the chimes of the Kremlin clock, transmitted by the radio. However, the twelfth stroke of the clock is not followed by the Russian state anthem as expected but instead the voice of a muezzin calling the faithful for prayer is heard, and both spacemen spread their prayer rugs, kneel down and start praying in Arabic. Thus according to the authors, in the future Islam will become the only religion in the world. Friendly and peaceful as the situation might seem it is hardly possible that plays of this sort may promote mutual understanding and friendship between people belonging to different religions.

Conclusion

Having analyzed the development of Russian political drama in the second half of the XXth and the beginning of the XXIst centuries I can state that the turn of the century was marked by its obvious outburst. "Over the last fifteen years, Russian drama came to embrace a vast array of styles and themes…such diversity was unthinkable prior to that summer in 1997 when a community of Russian writers stood poised to change the status quo. A time, it was said, when no one was writing plays of any interest," writes John Freedman in his essay *Contemporary Russian Drama: The Journey from Stagnation to a Golden Age*. Plays based on real facts, incorporating documentary materials, featuring political events and political figures not only of the historical past, but of the current present, and addressing most burning social issues of the day, turned over a new page in Russian theatre. Theatre of this kind started to articulate things that the official mass media prefer to keep silence about. The main conflict running throughout all of these plays is the conflict of the common man with the multifaceted society represented by state authorities, the president himself, the army, educational and penalty institutions, national communities and the mob, which reflects its general ill-being. The forms, styles and genres used are multiple; it can be the theatre of the absurd, an intellectual drama, a fairy tale, a farce, a naturalistic play or a verse drama. The very fact of the existence and development of political drama cannot be overestimated as it definitely shows the level of democratization in society. It has become possible to speak openly and sharply on the formerly forbidden subjects and criticize everything, government policy and the president. All this sounds quite optimistic, mainly in terms of social life and gives hope of its improvement. No wonder many foreign critics consider it to be a renaissance in Russian theatre as, for example, Emmanuel Grynszpan, who writes: "Some foreign theatergoers may think the nation that gave the world Chekhov and Gogol has rested on its laurels in recent years. Whatever collapse of confidence and creativity occurred in the Nineties has been replaced with something worthy of Konstantin Stanislavsky himself." However, in my opinion the aesthetic results of this process are much less auspicious. Unfortunately there are few really talented authors, and the talented ones have few really talented plays. Many playwrights seem to think that it is quite enough to refer to some topical question or to ridicule authorities using obscene language to write a good play. Just like in Soviet times it was beneficial to advertise official ideology it has become equally beneficial to run it down, so for some it is just another way of gaining recognition. So in spite of considerable creative potential, the appearance of young free thinking playwrights, new theatrical forms, and wonderful actors, Russian theatre has not yet fully overcome the crisis it found itself in at the beginning of the 1990s. The majority of new drama playwrights have not surpassed their Perestroika predecessors sometimes developing by far not the best aspects of their heritage. Even Birgit Beumers and Mark Lipovetsky, who in their comprehensive study of Russian new drama *Performing Violence* pay considerable tribute to its achievements can't but acknowledge that "...theatrical activity of "new drama" activists is marked by the signs of crisis. Thus, the last "new drama" festivals (2007-2008) did not bring about anything new and in fact repeated themselves" (368). In my opinion, we are still reaping the fruits of the long lasting period, when cultural ecology in the country was violated: due to ideological and aesthetical restrictions. Russian theatre, which at the beginning of the XXth century used to be in a vanguard of world theatre was thrown back, lost its originality and is now trying desperately to catch up, often repeating the forms and styles of Western drama. Russian dramatists seem to have forgotten the most characteristic feature of Russian literature, diagnosing the illness to give hope of revival and spiritual purification. The diagnosis is there—hopefully, spiritual purification is to come!

NOTES

1. A period of economic, political, and social stagnation in the Soviet Union, which began during the rule of Leonid Brezhnev (1964-1982) and continued under Iurii Andropov (1982-1984) and Konstantin Chernenko (1984-1985).
2. Such *agit-trials* were based on improvisation rather than a set script, and a common person, otherwise the victim of social injustice, could change his or her social mask and act as a judge of the oppressors. The spectators' attention was maintained both by the relevant political events themselves and the chance to express their attitude towards them. The success of such spectacles was determined not only by their mass scale but also by the absence of strict boundaries between performers and spectators.
3. For more details of this period see Tatyana Prokhorova and Vera Shamina "School for Democracy".
4. See, for example, Balotian, Ilmira, 2004, "O drame v sovremennom teatre: verbatim" ["On Drama in Modern Theatre: verbatim"].
5. This and all other translations from Russian are by the author.
6. On October 23, 2002 a seizure of the crowded *Dubrovka Theater* in Moscow, where the musical *Nord-Ost* was played by some 40 to 50 armed Chechens, took place.
7. The Beslan school siege started on the first of September 2004, lasted three days and involved the capture of over 1,100 people as hostages (including 777 children), ending with the death of over 380 people.

WORKS CITED

Asher, Byron. *In Russia's 'New Drama,' Chekhov Is Out, Grit Is In.* Web. Nov. 2014. <http://In_Russias_New_Drama_Chekhov_Is_Out_Grit_Is_In/1924988.html>.

Balotyan, Ilmira (2004). "O drame v sovremennom teatre: verbatim" ["On Drama in Modern Theatre: verbatim"]. Voprosi literaturi [Literary Studies], September-October, #5, 39-47.

Birgit Beumers and Mark Lipovetsky. *Performansi nasiliia. Literaturniie i teatralniie experimenty* [*Performing Violence. Literary and Theatrical Experiments of New Russian Drama*], Moscow: Novoye Literaturnoye Obozreniye, 2012.

Freedman John. "Contemporary Russian Drama: The Journey from Stagnation to a Golden Age". *Theatre Journal*. 62:3, October 2010. Web. Nov. 2014. <http://muse.jhu.edu/journals/tj/summary/v062/62.3.freedman.html>

Grynszpan, Emmanuel. Russia Now. Web. Nov. 2014. <http://www.telegraph.co.uk/sponsored/rbth/culture/8481583/Moscows-New-Drama-theatre.html>

Halpin, Tony. "World Agenda: play ridiculing Putin shows activists have lost their fear", The Times, April 16, 2012. Web. 24. Nov. 2014. <http://www.thetimes.co.uk/tto/news/world/agenda/article3385456.ece>

Istranin, Dmitrii. "Mi, vi, oni..." ["We, you, they"]. *Putin.Doc. Deviat revolutsionnykh p'ies.* [*Putin.Doc. Nine Revolutionary Plays*]. Tver: KOLONNA Publications, 2005: 129-75.

Malgin, Andrey. "Prisiadkin na tom svete". ["Prisiadkin in the Other World"]. *Putin.Doc. Deviat revolutsionykh p'ies.* [*Putin.Doc. Nine Revolutionary Plays*]. Tver: KOLONNA Publications, 2005. 37-129.

Nikolskaia, Alla. "Verbatim-unisex" ["Verbatim-unisex"]. *Kultura* [*Culture*], June 20-26, 2002.

Olaszec, Barbara. "Russkaya sovremennaia politicheskaia drama v otnoshenii k traditsii" ["Russian Modern Political Drama in Relation to Tradition"]. *Acta Universitatis Lodziensis, Folia Litteraria Rossica*, #5 2012: 164-71.

Tatyana Prokhorova and Vera Shamina. "School for Democracy". Spec. issue of *Comparative Drama*. 48.1-2 (2014): 59-75.

Rudnev, Pavel. "Etot ston u nas p'iesoi zoviotsia" ["This Moan We Call a Play"], *Putin.Doc. Deviat revolutsionnykh p'ies.* [*Putin.Doc. Nine Revolutionary Plays*]. KOLONNA Publications, 2005: 5-8.

❑❑❑

Island as Destination

RAMA KUNDU

I

Virginia Woolf: *To the Lighthouse* (1927)

'To Get on *To the Lighthouse*': The Exquisite Beacon

JOHN Harvey represents the typical readers' response when he admits: "the novel which I do go back to again and again is the one that I suppose everyone does, To the Lighthouse" ('Panel Discussion I', in Warner 125). Indeed, by general critical consensus, *To the Lighthouse* touches the acme of Virginia Woolf's excellence as a visionary and poetic mind expressing itself in a wonderful wealth of musical and visual images. What is the secret of this attraction?

On May 14, 1925, the day *Mrs. Dalloway* was published, Virginia Woolf noted in her *Diary* her desire to 'get on To the Lighthouse', and in another note on June 27, indicated that 'the sea was to be heard through it'. Is it the evocation of this superb music of the elements that counts for the attraction of the novel, the spell it casts upon a responsive reader?

After *Mrs Dalloway* the author leaves London behind, and goes ahead to a place far from the madding crowd of the capital, to a remote island by the Scottish coast, and places her characters by the sea there, and by doing so, according to Dorothy Brewster, "draws a magic circle around them" (Brewster 114). The story is set on an island. There is another smaller isle a little further away, from which the lighthouse sends its beams to the island, which contains the summer resort of the Ramsay family and their friends. It is not too close, but neither has it been rendered inaccessible. It is a quite reachable distance between the warm buzzing summerhouse and the distant, lone lighthouse.

This locale, including both the summerhouse beach and the lighthouse, a small island and a smaller isle, is supposed to have been based on an actual location and carries obvious autobiographical echoes. It is the Isle of Skye in Scotland. The house of the Ramsays is located on a Hebridean island, a group of islands west of Scotland; it is actually a replica of the Talland house of Woolf's father in St Ives which the family used as summer retreat from 1882 to 1892. Virginia was apparently fond of the house, and used to visit it along with her sister Vanessa long after their parents' death. Many details of the house, the garden, the sea and the lighthouse have been transcripted in the novel. The Godrevy lighthouse nearby is supposedly the original of the lighthouse in the story. Of course, in the story these 'actual' objects undergo an imaginative transfusion by means of passing through the luminous halo of the author's vision, and in the process get muted into a unique 'textual' place.

However, 'textual' though the island is, readers and critics have continued to guess about the exact or possible location of this charming textual island. David Daiches, in his *Virginia Woolf*, suggests it is possibly in the northwest of Scotland, though he is not absolutely sure. It can be amusing to remember that on 14 July 2009, the breaking news on the net was that the beach overlooking the lighthouse supposed to be the novel's original was sold at auction yesterday (13th July) for £80,000. Anyway, is it at all necessary to identify or 'map' the location? Or, alternatively, could we take it, as Brewster suggests, as a "composite one…or largely imaginary" (Brewster 114) place? In the first section Paul quotes the guidebook: "these islands being justly celebrated for their park-like prospects and the extent and variety of their marine curiosities" (*TL* 82); but Andrew Ramsay silently notes, with dismay, the inadequacy of this picknicker's approach to the place (*TL* 82).

Perhaps its real location is in the fond memory of the author's own summer days in a happier past. In this context Schaefer's sensitive response can be cited: "Beginning with an actual lighthouse which stands out in the sea, she (Woolf) quickly allies this real lighthouse with a spiritual one: an illuminated experience in the past which stands up out of the waste of time and sheds its glow on the present" (Schaefer 73).

In course of the narrative the lighthouse emerges as a loaded image, sending its radiant suggestions in multiple directions and thereby stirring multiple meanings.

James knows that both the 'silvery, misty-looking tower' of his childhood, and the 'stark and straight' tower of the present are true. The lighthouse serves as an aesthetic symbol, and conceptual signifier at multidimensional levels.

> The Lighthouse was then [in the past] a silvery, misty-looking tower with a yellow looking eye, that opened suddenly, and softly in the

> evening. Now—James looked at the Lighthouse. He could see the white-washed rocks, the tower, stark and straight; he could see that it was barred with black and white; he could see windows in it.... So that was the Lighthouse, was it? No, the other was also the Lighthouse. For nothing was simply one thing. The other Lighthouse was true too. (*TL* 202)

In this context one feels the aptness of Gregory Wilson's observation that the lighthouse "exists as the most enigmatic object in the novel" (Wilson 77).

Mrs Ramsay is sympathetic about their compulsive isolation, and thinks of giving some items to amuse the lighthouse keeper—"those poor fellows who must be bored to death sitting all day with nothing to do but polish the lamp and trim the wick and rake about on their scrap of garden.... For how would you like to be shut up for a whole month at a time, and possibly more in a stormy weather, upon a rock the size of a tennis lawn?" (*TL* 8-9). She finely, and rather lyrically sums up the situation to her daughters to convince them of the need of comfort to those poor people: "to have no letters or newspapers, and to see nobody; if you were married, not to see your wife, not to know how your children were...; to see the same dreary waves breaking week after week, and then a dreadful storm coming, and the windows covered with spray, and birds dashed against the lamp, and the whole place rocking, and not be able to put your nose out of doors for fear of being swept into the sea? How would you like that?" (*TL* 9).

Sometimes, awake in the darkness of night she thinks with an "impulse of terror" of the possible "destruction of the island and its engulfment in the sea" (*TL* 20). Yet the beauty resulting from the embrace of the island by the sea fascinates: "one watched, on the pale semicircular beach, wave after wave shedding again and again smoothly a film of mother-of-pearl" (*TL* 25).

From the very onset the lighthouse has been projected as a destination. The title itself suggests a direction—it is *to* the lighthouse, a smaller isolated island reaching out to another bigger one through its signal of light. The evening previous to the proposed trip to the Lighthouse Mrs Ramsay comes to the end of the story she had been reading out to little James. "'And that's the end', she said, and she saw in his eyes, as the interest of the story died away in them, something else take its place; something wondering, pale, like the reflection of a light, which at once made him gaze and marvel. Turning, she looked across the bay, and there, sure enough, coming regularly across the waves first two quick strokes, was the light of the Lighthouse. It had been lit.

> ...he kept looking back over his shoulder as Mildred carried him out, and she was certain that he was thinking, we are not going to the Lighthouse tomorrow; and she thought, he will remember that all his life." (*TL* 68)

It is as it were a destination, a place to go to, though not to stay on; and from the other island people wistfully look at it, want to make it to her; but the trip, intended though it had been in the beginning of the story, materializes only at the end after the lapse of ten years.

The subtitle of the third section could as well be 'one day on an island'. It is a micro-narrative of a journey and arrival, (both brief and smooth, no Odyssean hazards involved), for which the premise had already been laid out in the first section. It is, as it were, the journey's end, the novel's end, after which nothing can happen, Even Lily Briscoe, who does not physically undertake the trip to the lighthouse, and chooses to stay back instead on the bigger island, seems to be in unison with the rest, as she gives her final brush-stroke to her painting which was begun so long ago, indeed with the beginning of the story itself, but left unfinished until this morning. The trip brings about a reconcilement between an estranged parent and his resentful children; an empathic chord is touched between father and son, while the daughter suddenly discovers she can admire dad. The lighthouse opens the vista for envisioning life itself, in all its beauty and truth. The artist is happy that she has been able to execute her vision. The coincidence of the arrival at the lighthouse and the finishing of the painting is no accident. It is carefully contrived by the author.

In the third section of the novel the oldest member of the Ramsay family along with the youngest two, Mr Ramsay with his daughter Cam and son James, set off for the lighthouse. It is as it were, to keep an appointment made years back, when the beacon-isle could be seen only through the 'window' of the summer-house. In the meantime some of the appointees have already dropped off irrevocably, as 'time passed'. On the earlier occasion, in the first section, the little boy James, now a young man, had experienced deep disappointment as a proposed trip to the lighthouse had been cancelled, much like Virginia's own brother Adrian who had been denied the chance to go to the Godrevy lighthouse one summer morning in childhood. Now he is not even willing to go; and sets out only reluctantly.

David Daiches comments: "To reach the lighthouse is, in a sense, to make contact with a truth outside oneself, to surrender the uniqueness of one's ego to an impersonal reality" (Daiches 71). The arrival in the isle is made to coincide with Lily's finishing of the portrait she had started ten years ago. "Yes, she thought, laying down her brush..., I have had my vision." This is the last sentence of the book. The significance is obvious.

The locational paradigm of a sea-girdled small island—a familiar one in world literature—evocatively reinforces in the present context the theme of each person as an island, engulfed by its own stream [or sea?] of consciousness,—the persons/islands rendered isolated by the encircling sea/life. But the lighthouse (itself placed on an even smaller isle) sends its beams impartially to all. As David Daiches perceptively comments: "The lighthouse itself, standing lonely in the midst of the sea, is a symbol of the individual who is at once a unique being and a part of the flux of history" (Latham 71).

Indeed without the flux, the tossing waves, the island and the lighthouse have no existence. The sea and the island, that eternal duo, are entangled in embrace and battle; the sea embracing, lapping the isle, and the lighthouse "silver[ing] the rough waves".

The island and the lighthouse on it are still amidst the ever-restless waves, yet these are inseparable from the sea, which is 'pitiless, remorseless' like time. Yet it gives Mrs Ramsay, "this peace, this rest, this eternity" (*TL* 70). James, Cam, Mr Ramsay, and Lily back at home, all are at peace in the end as they reach the lighthouse; the other three literally, and Lily imaginatively, by envisioning and thus mentally participating in, the journey.

It is the one point of stability amidst the ceaseless flux of time. 'Time Passes'. But the lighthouse remains; and the journey though aborted once, can be, and has been made. Is it just atonement for one's past insensitivity? Or, is it something more? Drawing any such exclusive inference can be misleading. It is paradoxical and ambiguous: it is on the one hand epitome of both peace and stability, and on the other stern like remorseless, pitiless time; it is both misty and stark.

Sea and island also suggest the counterpoints of chaos and order; order amidst chaos. The lighthouse in a way symbolizes this order, as a stable point amidst the tossing waves. Seen in this perspective the dining room itself becomes a lighthouse; on the eve of Mrs Ramsay's dinner party: "Now all the candles were lit…inside the room there seemed to be order and dry land. …outside, a reflection in which things wavered and vanished, waterily" (*TL* 106). With the candles lit the party around the table seems to be order and dry land. People make the party on an island, having "their common cause against that fluidity out there" (*TL* 106). Later in the abandoned house "Listening (had there been any one to listen) from the upper rooms of the empty house only gigantic chaos streaked with lighting could have been heard tumbling and tossing, as the winds and waves disported themselves…" (*TL* 147). The Lighthouse continues tirelessly to send its beams into the nooks and chinks, on the walls, upon the dusty carpets of the now empty house. In the section 'Time Passes', which reads like a sustained lyric poem, the empty house has been subjected to the 'fertility', 'insensibility' of nature. The garden has gone wild. Birds have built inside the rooms and insects settled on the furniture. "The place was gone to rack and ruin. Only the Lighthouse beam entered the rooms for a moment, sent its sudden stare over bed and wall in the darkness of winter, looked with equanimity at the thistle and the swallow, the rat and the straw" (*TL* 150).

Towards the end of 'Time Passes', guests have arrived again, the house goes to sleep, with the curtains of darkness wrapping themselves over the house; and "the sigh of all the seas breaking in measure round the isles soothed them" (*TL* 155). While the waves break gently, "tenderly the light fell" (*TL* 155).

Thus the sea is also a harmonizer, and the sea and the island together make the spectrum, the 'luminous halo'. The sea lends the perspective, both artistic and philosophical. While looking at the island from the boat, Cam—"she had never seen it from out at sea before" (204)—sees it getting "very small…very distant" (207). Almost synchronically Lily recalls her past feeling "that she must be in love with the place" (208); she finds her perspective through the distant "blue haze" (225), into which the Lighthouse has "melted away".

As Mrs Ramsay looks enraptured at the lighthouse, "waves of pure delight race over the floor of her mind" (*TL* 72). The sleepers are soothed by "the sigh of all the seas breaking in measure round the isles" (155). Music arises from the clash of opposites; yet it is soothing. Is it because they are not really opposites, but complementary?

The sea can be the potential destroyer of the island as well as its protector. Irene Simon observes: "To Mr Ramsay, the sea is the enemy, and he defies the flood from his spit of land" (Simon 79). Mr Ramsay, ambling along the lawn, comes to the edge and while looking out on the bay beneath, starts his interior monologue, in which the sea and the edge of land become signifier of his lone intellectual pursuit: "It was his fate,…to come out thus on a spit of land which the sea is slowly eating away, and there to stand, like a desolate sea-bird, alone…to stand on his little ledge facing the dark of human ignorance, how we know nothing, and the sea eats away the ground we stand on…" (*TL* 50). To Mrs Ramsay the waves falling on the beach also beat a "measured and soothing tattoo to her thoughts" and repeat consolingly "I am guarding you—I am your support" (*TL* 20); but sometimes she can also hear in the sound of the waves crashing upon the island shore "a ghostly roll of drums remorselessly beat the measure of life", it can make her "think of the destruction of the island and its engulfment in the sea" and warn her "that it was all ephemeral…—this sound which had been obscured and concealed under the other sounds suddenly thundered hollow in her ears and made her look up with an impulse of terror" (*TL* 20).

The individual itself is but a speck of land amidst the vast sea of life. "Indeed the individual feels his nothingness in front of the sea" (Simons 79), because, as Lily feels, it seems "to outlast by a million years the gazer…" (25). To Mr Ramsay, sometimes "the little island seemed pathetically small, half swallowed up in the sea". He would murmur with a sigh, "poor little place" (*TL* 76).

At the same time the piece of land with its light-tower also epitomizes stability in microcosmic manifestation. Gregory Wilson observes: "…the third section of the novel does indeed provide some spatial and temporal resolution. Mr Ramsay and his son and daughter finally make it to the lighthouse, and Lily finally completes her painting. But the only way either of these resolutions is possible is through the Lighthouse itself, …it stands as the *one entity* within the entire novel unaffected by the passage of time. At the beginning it stands, forbidding and austere, to the sight of Lily and the Ramsays; it remains stable through the ten years…; and it appears to James as an entity unaffected by the fading years, if not immune to change altogether…" (Wilson 77).

The time frame of the novel is the decade between 1910 and 1920, which, though begins in a climate of peace and stability, eventually involves change, decadence, death; already a change has taken place, owing to one big war which has taken its toll even from this house. One of the younger Ramsays, Andrew, has been killed in the war. On the other hand, as Wilson explains: "We feel here a certainty of unshifting conditions…the Lighthouse stands relatively unchanged, unaltered, the single item of stability in the book.… It is only when the characters have attained the Lighthouse, either physically or spiritually, that they are able to slow the passage of time enough to preserve moments of reality…" (Wilson 78). "...the center of temporal stasis represented by the Lighthouse" (Wilson 79). "…the Lighthouse…represents temporal stability, even if the characters who approach it are changed by the forces around them and impose the change upon the Lighthouse they see; and the attainment of its shores does allow the characters to attain a measure of that stability and permanence for themselves" (Wilson 80).

At the same time, the lighthouse means so many more things: "the path the eye traverses in seeing is compared to the ray sent out by a lighthouse. Thus Lily Briscoe sees William Bankes gazing with love at Mrs Ramsay and 'looking along his beam she added to it her different ray'…these various rays sent out by the lighthouses of the characters' minds" (Schaefer 73). Apart from this, a character can also partake something of the lighthouse or the island.

In a way Mrs Ramsay, though she casts her warmth and caring consideration upon everybody around, is like the lone lighthouse at the depth of her consciousness or psyche. "She could be herself, by herself. And that was what now she often felt the need of—to think; to be silent; to be alone." At the same time she is the centre, the focal point, the pivot holding the diverse elements together. She finds it pleasant to be alone, not to have to think, to be herself.… She feels a sense of triumph over life (Brewster 167), and, pausing, looks out to meet the stroke of the lighthouse, "the long steady stroke, the last of the three, which was her stroke" (*TL* 70). She looks at the beam, and slowly gets into an ecstasy: "watching it with fascination, hypnotised, as if it were stroking with silver fingers some sealed vessel in her brain whose bursting would flood her with delight, she had known happiness, exquisite happiness, intense happiness, and it silvered the rough waves a little more brightly, as daylight faded, and the blue went out of the sea and it rolled in waves of pure lemon which curved and swelled and broke upon the beach and the ecstasy burst in her eyes and waves of pure delight raced over the floor of her mind and she felt, 'It is enough! It is enough!'" (*TL* 72).

During her epiphanic vision the third stroke from the lighthouse: "seemed to her like her own eyes meeting her own eyes, searching as she alone could search into her mind and heart, purifying out of existence... any lie. She praised herself in praising the light, without vanity, for she was stern, she was searching, she was beautiful like that light" (*TL* 70). She looks at the long steady light, and feels "an irrational tenderness" (*TL* 70) as if it were a part of her own.

John Graham touches the point tangentially in his essay 'Time in the Novels of Virginia Woolf':

> The lighthouse is the central symbol of the book, and what it means depends on who is looking at it: it has no single limited meaning, hence its power as a symbol. Its relation to Mrs Ramsay is of crucial importance, for Mrs Ramsay has the power to see.... Although she sits in her room and undergoes the mystical experience of becoming the thing she looks at, the lighthouse, she nevertheless recognizes that its meaning is paradoxical: it is 'so much her, yet so little her'.... This makes it an objective correlative for Mrs Ramsay's vision. (in Latham 33)

Schaefer comments: "The real lighthouse of the novel, therefore, is the one which Mrs Ramsay carefully sets glowing and which illuminates a space of life even after her death. This illumination becomes a triumph of the human spirit" (Schaefer 78).

Some critics have ushered in biographical sidelights to probe the implications of the lighthouse. According to Gordon: "Virginia Woolf thought biography should leave something to the imagination.... When she composes her portrait of her mother...she asked, first, what was her mother to herself? It was an inspired stroke to let the beam of the lighthouse catch her, in a rare moment, alone. The scene is deliberately understated, unanalyzed, a model of biographic tact" (61). But perhaps it is more than just 'biographic tact'; the lighthouse emerges to be such a rich symbol.

Even Mr Ramsay, seen from a particular angle, can be shown to bear semblance to a lighthouse—

> It was his power, his gift, suddenly to shed all superfluities, to shrink and diminish so that he looked barer and felt sparer...stand[ing] on his little ledge facing the dark of human experience, how we know nothing and the sea eats away the ground we stand on...he kept even in that desolation a vigilance.... (*TL* 72)

At the end a unity is achieved in which converge the past and the present, the living and the dead; "...the completion of the proposed journey to the lighthouse is a re-membering (in both senses of the word) that draws

Mr Ramsay, James, and Cam together in unprecedented solidarity" (Jarerd F. Green 133). On the appointed morning James and Cam are not ready. They are reluctant. But finally when they reach the Lighthouse (*TL* 202), though an 'other' than the image retained in their childhood memory, and registered there through distant perception, already the signification has been made.

There has been identification between the voyager and the goal; so the journey, seen on another plane, becomes a journey within and into one's own inner self. The Lighthouse is distant, stark, a destination. Yet it is also part of one's own inner self—"the long steady stroke was her stroke" (*TL* 70)—as Mrs Ramsay had known in a flash during her epiphanic vision one summer evening. Even without physically going there she had had her voyage done, the journey made, the destination reached. Thus journeying to it is also, at another level, a journey within.

Finally, the clue to the extraordinary charm of the novel lies indeed, among other factors, to its being an excellent illustration of the process by which an empirical island can be turned into a rich symbol, 'silvering' every object and every mind within the periphery.

II

Onward to the Remotest Islet: A Destructive Destination

D.H. Lawrence: 'The Man who Loved Islands'

Whereas in Virginia Woolf's novel we find people on an island responding to the beckoning of a small isle, and finding a kind of fulfillment thereby, Lawrence's story also involves a journey from a small island, to a smaller one, and finally the smallest; but which proves destructive for the recluse.

Fiona Becket observes: "Lawrence is one of the key short-story writers of the modernist period.... The stories that constitute the collections are central to an understanding of Lawrence's major preoccupations, such as his exploration of the relationships between men and women; the instinctive life; the realization of self-awareness; the examination of cultural, as well as personal, dissolution and the related critique of Western civilization as misdirected in its pursuit of ideal values; the multi-directional exploration of mythic and religious themes..." (Fiona Becket 91). 'The Man who Loved Islands', one of the author's own favorite stories, is a case in point.

'The Man who Loved Islands' has been claimed by David Ellis in his biography of Lawrence as "the most philosophical fiction he ever wrote" (Ellis 31). It is the story of a man's gradual withdrawal from the wider world of all living creatures, human and animal, into a cocoon of his own self. It is a paradoxical retreat which would eventually destroy the recluse.

The original target of the story, is supposed to be Sir Compton Mackenzie (1883-1972),—though Lawrence had subsequently denied it—the prolific and popular novelist, biographer, historian, born into a theatrical family, who had all along proudly proclaimed his Scottish alignment, and pursued activity in the Scottish nationalist line. Capri, the Italian island, was his favorite nook, where he lived between 1913 and 1920, accompanied by his wife Faith; in his later years also he returned to the place. Two of his novels bear the record of his observations about the island: *Vestal Fire* (1927) and *Extraordinary Women* (1928). From 1920 to 1923 he lived in the Channel islands, Herm and Jethou. In 1928 he found a new place in the Western Isles, namely the Isle of Barra, where he settled and built a spacious house. Following his death in 1972, he was buried in Barra, near his house. His most popular comic novel *Whisky Galore* (1947) was an island story set in the Hebrides (the same as Woolf's setting for *To the Lighthouse*), and based on a real event of 1941 in Eriskay, an island visible from his Barra house where a US-bound cargo-vessel, named *S.S. Cabinet Minister*, carrying 28,000 cases of Scotch Whiskey had stuck. The consequence can be guessed, leading to the legendary raid of the wreck by the local islanders.

In view of Lawrence's habitual practice of using personal acquaintances as material for stories, Middleton Murry for instance in 'Smile', and 'The Border-Line', it is not unlikely that Lawrence should have used certain data of Mackenzie's life, albeit obliquely, which were so well-known at the time of writing the story, as raw material for his narrative. But the created artifact far transcends the starting point, in case there was such one. And the finished product, in spite of the rich vein of irony underlying the narration, particularly in the first part, does not read like a personal satire by any count; and readers of today, without any inkling about the personal factor, would rather enjoy the story as an impressive symbolic text than otherwise.

Critics like Coroneos and Tate, who have rightly described the beginning of the story as "the fairy-tale opening" (112), furthermore claim, "the fabulous-symbolic mode...wilfully ignores the claims of gritty naturalism. It moves with ease between levels of significance and information, effortlessly integrating the most occult concepts with everyday gossip and malice concerning Lawrence's immediate acquaintance" (112-13).

The story has been subjected to psychoanalytical criticism by Ben Stoltzfus, John Turner and David Willbern respectively. While according to Stoltzfus the journey of the protagonist from one island to other increasingly remoter islands are in tune with the Lacanian theme of gradual psychic withdrawal into the primeval state of consciousness, Turner analyses his obsession and regressive journey as the flight of a schizophrenic individuality. Willbern studies him in the Freudian light of 'ambivalence'.

Jill Franks, on the other hand, reads it as the author's self-parody. Franks suggests a biographical explanation that Lawrence was aware "of the dangers of isolation inherent in his various island schemes, which were the successors to the aborted Rananim planned with Bertrand Russell in 1915. In 1926, he wrote 'The Man Who Loved Islands' as an allegory and a brilliant self-parody." The three islands, according to her, correspond to Lawrence's three conflicting ideals to which he held on all along: these were, namely, Rananim or 'intentional community', personal fulfillment through sexual union, and independence from society. Franks further argues that Cathcart's three island experiences offer a "self-reflexive commentary…on Lawrence's ideals and his *Weltanschauung*".

However, one cannot afford to overlook the fact that Cathcart represents failure on all the three counts. Lawrence, as Franks herself has admitted, was a man who believed in reaching out, in making connections instead of withdrawal and self-isolation.

The story opens with the characteristic simplicity and quick but balanced pace of a fable, as well as the suggestion of the remoteness, the obscurity of a fairy tale.

> There was a man who loved islands. He was born on one, but it didn't suit him, as there were too many other people on it, besides himself. He wanted an island all of his own: not necessarily to be alone on it, but to make it a world of his own. (Lawrence 97)

Fiona Becket observes: "As 'fables' they draw attention to Lawrence's highly successful handling of the form and demonstrable authorial control. At their best each is a finely crafted text..." (Fiona Becket 91). Indeed, with perfect ease the storyteller moves on, interweaving the particular individual case of a man, with the generalizations about islands and their relationship with humans. Thus the focus on the particular in the first paragraph is balanced by the general metaphysical speculative, albeit ironical tone of the second.

> "An island, if it is big enough, is no better than a continent. It has to be really quite small, before it *feels* like an island. And this story will show how tiny it has to be, before you can presume to fill it with your own personality". (97)

The celebrated 'monarch of all I survey' type feeling is apparently undermined! The narrator's preference is for the small islet rather than a big thing. Otherwise he thinks one does not get the 'feel' of the 'insulation'.

Or can we be sure? Because, from the very beginning there is also a barely hidden tone of irony which also indicates the narrator's self-distancing from his protagonist. Coroneos and Tate remark:

> ...the bathetic is also figured in the structure of the narrative: the idealists are constantly recontextualised, each context part of a process of reduction, rather like the quest of the man who loved islands for an ever-smaller island.... In many of the quest tales, in fact, the structure is a mischievous degenerative spiral, a progressive dismantling of idealism, as if *Pilgrim's Progress* meets *Candide*. (116)

The particular man is mentioned as, as if half-mockingly, 'our islander'. Lawrence's islander closely resembles a colonial settler, 'the Master' of the imperial era; furthermore, he is a 'combo' figure—Odysseus-Selkirk-Crusoe rolled into one; and that too not by compulsion like those cultural icons, but by his own choice.

Yet the story touches the level of the superb in course of 'our islander's gradual regression to the smallest island. After having arrived and settled down in his third island, and having disposed even the sheep he gets "dim" "like some strange, ethereal animal" (120). He is barely conscious of the circumstances and the possible eventualities, in this bare, stark, puny island.

> Only he still derived satisfaction from being alone, absolutely alone, with the space soaking into him. The grey sea alone, and the footing of his sea-washed island. No other contact. Nothing human to bring its horror into contact with him. Only space, damp, twilit, sea-washed space! This was the bread of his soul. (120)

And at the end it is simply awesome, when the lone enfeebled terrified man stares stupefied at the whiteness of his now "unrecognizable island"

(124). He becomes frenzied. The man's withdrawal from island to island had been motivated by a desire for isolation. But at the end we find him eager for "the wink of a sail" which, in the earlier days would have maddened him with anger. It becomes too serious for satire or too grim for irony.

This is ironical in the sense that the desired destination ultimately proves disastrous, and not desired or desirable as it had initially appeared. "The man" had sought islands because he wanted to "make a world of his own". He is "one who loves an island for its insulation" (97). He would be the "one egg, and one only" in the "nest" that is the island.

The first island that he acquires is not very far, 'not in the remote oceans' (97). It is quite cosy, home-like, manageable, 'four miles' in all, all complete with a dwelling house, a small farmhouse and three cottages, primrose flowers on the little glades and blackthorn bushes up the steep rocks. From the edge of the island other bigger and smaller islands can be seen in different directions, which are also his possession. While locating this cluster of islands, the narrator comments: "Thus it seems that even islands like to keep each other company" (98).

The seasons roll on from spring through summer to autumn presaging winter. "The island, your island, cowered dark, holding away from you. You could feel, down in the wet, somber hollows, the resentful spirit coiled upon itself, like a wet dog coiled in gloom, or a snake" (98). In the night "you felt that your island was a universe, infinite and old as the darkness; not an island at all, but an infinite dark world where all the souls from all the other bygone nights lived on, and the infinite distance was near" (98-99). Incidentally, who is this 'you'? Is it the reader, or the islander? Is the narrator addressing/imagining the islander as an intimate second person? In his self-chosen insulation the persona continues his interior monologue, projecting his own self as the sole addressee. Or can it be the hint of a growing schizophrenia, which has been there in 'our islander' from the very start? The use of the second person in this context lends a touch of generalisation and universalisation to a particular situation of a particular individual.

Here we have metaphysical speculations on 'Time' in poetic articulation, which is the hallmark of Lawrence's style.

> Strangely, from your little island in space, you were gone forth into the dark, great realms of time, where all the souls that never die veer and swoop on their vast, strange errands. The little earthly island has

> dwindled, like a jumping-off place, into nothingness, for you have jumped off, you know not how, into the dark wide mystery of time, where the past is vastly alive, and the future is not separated off. (99)

This is certainly not satire, one must admit,—this 'dark wide mystery of time'.

At this point the narration takes a leap into metaphysical speculations about time and space, the hyperreality of space and the 'terrors' of time; the perception of time and space in inverse ratio. The particular strangeness of an island location involved, as it were, the proportionate inflation and diminution of time and space; just the constriction/confinement in space leads to the terrifying awareness of an immense time. "This is the danger of becoming an islander. When, in the city, you…dodge the traffic… you are quite safe from the terrors of infinite time…. But once isolate yourself on a little island in the sea of space, and the moment begins to heave and expand in great circles…in the timeless world, where the chariots of the so-called dead dash down the old streets of centuries…. The souls of all the dead are alive again, and pulsating around you. You are out in the other infinity" (99).

Feeling increasingly uneasy in his little space washed by the vast sea of 'Time', he begins to pay more attention to the material detail as a sort of remedial measure, and as a means of furthering his mission of making a perfect happy isle.—all complete with a butler, a housekeeper, an ever busy carpenter, a bailiff with two farm-hands, the skipper with wife and son, a mason; so that before long "it was a quiet, busy, little world" (101). And the islander becomes "the Master" (101) to everyone. For a time it is an ideal situation as "The Master was no tyrant...he was a delicate, sensitive, handsome Master, who wanted everything perfect and everybody happy. Himself, of course, to be the fount of this happiness and perfection" (101-02).

In a tongue-in-the-cheek manner the narrator reminds us of the egoistic element behind this façade of idealism. "Well, it was ideal. The Master was no tyrant…[he] wanted everything perfect and everybody happy. Himself, of course, to be the fount of this happiness and perfection" (101-02). He becomes almost a god as it were, to his small domain. Ironically, however, he is not really liked by them. Here Lawrence has his own theory to offer: general goodwill is felt to be a sort of insult to its object, and therefore, breeds a malice: "Surely general goodwill is a form of egoism, that it should have such a result!" (103). Very soon the project flounders, following heavy financial loss, and other accompanying misfortunes,—the death of the cow, for instance, or the sickness among men and pigs. The people also fall out against one another, because they were not contented as they were *not* islanders. "Yet the island was so lovely. When there was a scent of honeysuckle and the moon brightly flickering down on the sea, then even the grumblers felt a strange nostalgia for it. It set you yearning, with a wild yearning; perhaps for the past, to be far back in the mysterious past of the island, when the blood had a different throb. Strange floods of passion came over you, strange violent lusts and imaginations of cruelty. The blood and the passion and the lust which the island had known. Uncanny dreams, half-dreams, half-evocated yearnings" (107). Consequently "the Master himself began to be a little afraid of his island" (107).

It should be noted that the island exerts its weird influence only on 'our islander', and not on the employees, subjects in his 'monarchy'. The schizophrenic man loves and fears the same thing,—his island. His response to the place, which had been complex from the start, becomes more mixed. Slowly but surely by degrees the island becomes an "enemy" (108) in his perception. "The island itself seemed malicious" (106), bent upon destroying all his dreams. At the end of the third year, with increasing loss, and unmistakable evidences of treachery he feels: "The island was still mysterious and fascinating. But it was also treacherous and cruel, secretly, fathomlessly malevolent. In spite of all its fair show of white blossom and bluebells, and the lovely dignity of foxgloves bending their rose-red bells, it was your implacable enemy" (108).

Yet the master still loves it, "but with a touch of rancor now" (108). By the end of the fourth year "he wanted to get rid of it, as a man who wants a divorce at any cost" (109). By the middle of the fifth year he can manage to transfer it, though at considerable loss to himself.

Compelled to move, the islander moves on to the smaller island still in his possession instead of going back to the mainland, with just five of his former retinue. It is very small, just 'a hump of rock in the sea', and took only twenty minutes to cover. "Still it was an island" (109), and "the Master was still the master" (110).

The beautiful poetic description appropriately brings out the islander's rapture: "Yet it was an island. Always, always underneath among the rocks the Celtic sea sucked and washed and smote its feathery greyness" (110). It is "like the last point in space" (110); it is haunted by no ghosts of the past; there is only the sea with its noises, smell, and fog. For a time he is almost happy here. "The days went by, and the nights, without desire, without ennui" (111).

There has been a significant change in 'our islander', which has its impact on his perception of this second island: As he changes inwardly, holding more aloof from the others around, his island also dwindles proportionally.

> The island was no longer a 'world'. It was a sort of refuge. The islander no longer struggled for anything. He had no need. It was as if he and his few dependents were a small flock of sea-birds alighted on this rock, as they travelled through space, and keeping together without a word. The silent mystery of the travelling birds. (111)

The islander wonders if this 'stillness from all desire' (111) is happiness. He says to himself: "I am turned into a dream. I feel nothing, or I don't know what I feel. Yet it seems to me I am happy" (111). Sometimes he goes to the mainland, but feels glad to go back to 'his island'.

But the bliss does not last long. He gets involved with the widow's daughter who used to assist him in drawing up his manuscript. "It was the automatism of sex that had caught him", against his wishes. Though he marries the girl as she had become pregnant, and waits till the baby is born, the island has already become a humiliating prison for him, and "he was meditating escape" (113). After having made necessary arrangements for the mother and child, for whom the only response he registers is—"the millstone tied round his neck", he goes ahead towards north, for his third island. Already some months ago, he had bought an island at an auction, "a few acres of rock away", on the outer fringes of the isles. Difficult to access.

> It was low, it rose low out of the great ocean. There was not a building, not even a tree on it. Only northern sea-turf, a pool of rain-water, a bit of sedge, rock and sea-birds. Nothing else. Under the weeping wet western sky...the grey sea sucking angrily among the rocks. (115)

He was pleased with the place. "This was indeed an island" (115). Now he wants very little. A simple hut is built for him near the flat shingle bay; a boat brings a bed, a table and chairs, a few books, a supply of fuel and food. Her is glad at the bareness, not even trees or bushes. Now he does not like trees even: "They stood up like people, too assertive" (117). "His bare, low-pitched island in the pale blue sea was all he wanted" (117). He stops reading books. The island is so small that while walking among the rocks and turf of his small domain, he would be always coming "to the ceaseless, restless sea" (117). He does not want to hear voices, even his own. He detests the bleating sheep, 'hideous and gross', which he soon ships off. "He wanted only to hear the whispering sound of the sea, and the sharp cries of the gulls, cries that came out of another world to him. And best of all, the great silence" (117). He has been heading towards a complete withdrawal through a complete denial of life, negation of its sights and sounds. Only the elements—the water and air, the sky; and the sea. The birds from distant regions belong to the sky.

The cat, the only residue from the previous island, another world, also disappears one day. Then begins the rain. He would just watch from his hut the rain, the dark rocks, the sea. Sea-birds of all sorts arrived. But his former curiosity to know their names no longer worked. Then the birds also leave; the days shorten; the world growing eerie. On the rare occasion of the boat bringing in the mail he is annoyed; he does not open the letters which seemed repulsive intrusion from the outside. Gradually he was losing hold. He cannot think clearly or feel. "Only he still derived his single satisfaction from being alone, absolutely alone, with the space soaking into him, a counterpoint to Coleridge's famous mariner, alone on a wide, wide sea, and not at peace with himself at all. The grey sea alone, and the footing of his sea-washed island. No other contact. Nothing human to bring its horror into contact with him. Only space, damp, twilit, sea-washed space! This was the bread of his soul" (120). He feels glad when the sea is risen under a storm, because no one could intrude now. "He always liked the sea to be heavily rolling and tearing. Then no boat could get him. It was like eternal ramparts round his island" (120). In course of his gradual withdrawal he comes to a stage when he cannot endure the sight of printed words. It seems too vulgar. He erases the last bit of lettering in his cabin. When the cat disappears at last he feels rather glad.

He slips by degrees into a state of semi-consciousness, half-awareness. He seems to have grown an obsession about possible intrusion. If he sees a sail in the distance "a strange malevolent anger passed over his features" (120). Apart from this he seems to have lost all other motivation. Prowling about his island in the rain, he does not know what he is looking at, nor what he wants to see. He becomes increasingly weak, sick. Disintegration has set in; and this is in tune with the external nature. Then the cold came. "The island was freezing.... The cold frightened him" (121). The 'dull, deathly cold' is accompanied by snow. The birds disappear, and with them the last signs of life leave. The man feels a "cruel satisfaction" in the thought that "Soon…in all these regions nothing will be alive" (121). He himself is getting weaker, but is not conscious of his condition. When he feels ill he takes some milk and malt from his store, and thus manages to survive. Through the night there are rumbling of thunder and flashes of lightning; in the morning it is all white; a series of death-images follow to accentuate the desolation and the oncoming disaster; the snow-fall through the '*dead* air'; the flavor of death all around: "The sea ate at the whiteness of the *corpse-like* land" (121; emphasis added). Next morning he gets up in the "*dead* cold" (122); the hut is covered with snow; it is as high as his breast. Trying to look above and beyond it, "he felt the *dead* wind slowly driving, saw the snow-powder lift and travel like a *funeral* train" (122). In the "awful, *dead* wind", amidst "*white*, *lifeless* surroundings" (122), he desperately tries to reach his boat; because an important realization has burst in: "If he was to be shut in, it must be by his own choice, not by the mechanical power of the elements" (122). It is man alone confronting elemental nature and the confrontation proves too much. Nature appears in the form of a brute force; he persuades himself: "He must conquer the snow, this new, white *brute* force which had accumulated against him" (122). "The wet rocks were *brutally* black" (123). In the silence of the dark night "it seemed he could hear the *panther-like* dropping of infinite snow" (123). Following a night of howling wind and ceaseless thud of snow, he comes out, or rather digs out of his snow-covered door to find "his island was gone" (123) under rising white hills, and "he was sickened and overcome" (123). "The elements! The elements! His mind repeated the word dumbly. You can't win against the elements" (123).

Stranded in his now "unrecognizable island" he would "pretend to imagine" a sail coming by, a sight which had been so repugnant to him in the former days.

At the end he is helplessly waiting for the imminent and inescapable death. Perhaps, after all, no man is an island, or can be one! Is that the proposition of Lawrence? Lawrence's islander is a perfectionist. So when he looks for loneliness that also becomes an absolutist search. But ultimately this turns out to be a self-defeating pursuit. It is perhaps significant that each of the three (a mysterious number) islands has initially charmed him but eventually has been perceived as enemy.

His name is used only once; otherwise he is mentioned as 'the islander' or 'our islander', like the name and surname. The near anonymity helps the story to attain the mythical plane. Indeed, the mythical overtone is unmistakable, which lends a special dimension to the story. At the beginning, which is early spring, (—spring in the Biblical garden of Eden) the first island is beautiful, perfectly in tune with the eager happy mood of 'our islander'.

> Our islander loved his island very much. In early spring, the little ways and glades were a snow of blackthorn, a vivid white among the Celtic stillness of close green and grey rock, blackbirds calling out in the whiteness their first long, triumphant calls. After the blackthorn and the nestling primroses came the blue apparition of hyacinths, like elfin lakes and slipping sheets of blue, among the bushes and under the glade of trees. And many birds with nests you could peep into, on the island *all your own.* Wonderful what a great world it was! (98; emphasis added)

Almost an Edenic paradise, much like the island of Circe. But spring does not last. In the summer that follows the flowers disappear, the corns ripen; soon it is autumn with its brief fullness, and ethereal beauty, when the moon itself emerges like another island. "...it was autumn, the oat-sheaves lying prone, the great moon, another island, rose golden out of the sea, and rising higher, the world of the sea was white" (98).

The cycle of seasons go on in the remote isolated spits of land as in a great mythic world. Spring leads to summer; summer yields to autumn; before long autumn ends with rain, and winter sets in with its dark skies and dampness. Now the island changes and assumes mythic properties. It does not seem genial and friendly any more, but looks distant and ancient. It seems mythic and primordial.

Lawrence touches the mythical level as he goes on registering the islander's growing perception of this impalpable universe in terms of an endless expanse of 'Time' (99). The past—mythical, primordial—seems to come up and engulf the present. This wind from the past and even more ancient past fills the islander with unease, particularly during the night time. The uncanny memories of an uncanny past haunts this man who "had reduced himself to a single point in space...a point being that which has neither length nor breadth..." (99-100).

Here we have a lone man face to face with elemental nature, which can prove too much for a solitary islander in this vast sea of life.

III

'Terra Incognita', 'to find the Unfindable': 'the Island not Found'

Umberto Eco *The Island of the Day Before* (1988).

The Island of the Day Before opens with the exclamation of an outcast, who has been forced into a situation too extraordinary even for an outcast. The very opening lines register the uniqueness of the situation.

> I take pride in my humiliations and as I am to this privilege condemned, almost I find joy in an abhorrent salvation. I am, I believe, alone of all our race, the only man in human memory to have been shipwrecked and cast up upon a deserted ship.

The book begins with the typical situation to start off an island fiction of the imperial-voyaging adventuring-exploring era; it is the paradigmatic spring-board for launching a typical species of the genre: that of a man "shipwrecked and cast up" (*IDB* 1). The departure from the paradigm becomes evident as soon as the author mentions the location of the 'cast up'—that it is not an island, but "upon a deserted ship" (*IDB* 1). It has not been his own choice. "Casale he had entered of his own choice, to prevent others from entering: he had been cast up on the *Daphne*, and yearned only to leave it" (*IDB* 45).

Roberto della Griva, an Italian youth from the wrecked English ship *Amaryllis*, eventually gets stuck up in *Daphne*, a grounded Dutch ship in the South Pacific, the favorite zone of the explorers and the 'desert island' writers. The year is 1643. The English ship Roberto boards follows the typical pattern of voyage in those days: "In search of supplies, the ship sailed up the coast of Chile to the west and anchored at a desert island..." (*IDB* 205). "And the ship continued its voyage, moving through sepia seas" (*IDB* 208). In the way of adding to the plausibility, the narrator also refers to real sea voyage tales (*IDB* 244; 298) as well as fantasy sea voyage tales (*IDB* 251), which were already in currency by the time. For instance, the reference to Tasman's voyage, the route of which collides with Roberto's own at points: "Abel Tasman, setting out from Batavia, more or less during the months of our story, had... also arrived at a land that he called Van Diemen, which today we know as Tasmania; but since he, too, was seeking the Solomon Islands, he kept the southern shore of that land on his left, never imagining that beyond it lay a continent a hundred times greater, and he ended up southeast of New Zealand, flanked it to the northeast and, abandoning it, reached the Tongas. Thus he arrived by and large where the *Daphne* was, I believe, but there, too, he passed between the coral reefs and headed for New Gunea…" (*IDB* 244). Or, the cannibal episode,—which reads like a page taken from the fantastic account of *Travels* (1356-67) by Sir John Mandeville—black men, after eating up white sailors on board, proceeding to taste the ship assuming it to be a living creature, delivering longboats (*IDB* 251).

The ship Roberto has chanced to land upon turns out to be a sailing ship, which is well-stocked but abandoned. It is in the tropical zone. The ship is stocked well with provisions, but appears to have been abandoned mysteriously. There is apparently no danger. But the young man, Roberto, cannot swim; and he is completely alone, an outcast on board. He has been a shipwreck during a storm; latched up on a raft, he has floated up to reach this strange ship. Thus the ship itself becomes the epitome and replica of an island, albeit a floating one: "on the lower deck he had found a miniature island" (*IDB* 68).

In a sense the book is a period-piece registering the cultural obsession of the era with sea-voyage tales, be they real or fantasia. The narrative frankly draws upon the popular paradigm of the typical sea-voyage tales of the era. It is the cultural climate of the Age of Exploration that flavors the narration and conditions the mindset of the narrator within the narrative of this metanarrative: the lure of the new era—the thrill and excitement about the prospect of knowing the 'Very New' world (*IDB* 187). It also aptly highlights the importance of islands in this explorative venture which had fired the imagination of Europe like anything. The explorers' favorite zone was the Pacific, and especially the South Pacific. Mazarin explains to Roberto, the would-be-passenger on the *Amaryllis*: "In the United Provinces, in England, Portugal, and Spain, there is no noble family that does not have one son off at sea making his fortune....[But] whereas we know enough perhaps of the New World, we know little of the Very New" (*IDB* 187). He is also reasonably anxious about the enterprise of possible rivals in the zone: "After the discovery of a western passage to the Moluccas, this whole vast unexplored zone is at hazard, extending from the western shores of the American continent to the last eastern outcrops of Asia. I refer to the ocean called the Pacific, as the Portugese have named it, in which surely lies the Austral Terra Incognita, of which surely lies Austral Terra Incognita, of which only a few islands are known, a few hazy coasts, but still enough for us to assume that it contains fabulous riches. And now, for some time, too many adventurers who do not speak our language have been swarming over those waters" (*IDB* 187).

The narrative smells, as it were, of brine, mist, feel of the water-air-land (not far from the watery location of the narrator), and above all fascination for the yet unmapped 'virgin' islands, which often stir the micro-narrator (Eco himself being the metanarrator who 'edits' the scraps of notes left by Roberto on the board of *Daphne*) to lyrical bursts. Roberto even imagines the possibility of islands even in the moon. "Sometimes I look at the Moon, and I imagine that those darker spots are caverns, cities, islands, and the places that shine are those where the sea catches the light of the sun like the glass of a mirror" (*IDB* 80). The moon is envisioned by him as the replication of the earth, and the replication includes the 'island' and the 'sea', as the most important items of the lunar topography in the dreamer's perception.

Understandably, the castaway was a familiar figure of those times which upheld and almost made a cult of voyaging, exploration and 'discovery' of new lands, which usually/actually meant islands; shipwreck was a common phenomenon during those early days of navigation in the far seas. As the narrator of Eco's book conjectures: "I imagine that in those days, and on those seas, more ships were wrecked than returned safely home" (*IDB* 14). Thus, through a quite realistic accident he arrives at a fantasy ship.

Roberto knows too, like the European elite of his times: "If he was destined to remain a castaway for a long time, he had to maintain good manners and not become bestialized" (*IDB* 63). However, Roberto is a 'castaway' with a difference. There is an island not far away; "he could discern, about a mile away, the form of the island, the palm trees along its shore stirred by a breeze" (*IDB* 3); this too corresponds to the familiar skyline of the typical desert island fiction of the imperial centuries. But in the present case the castaway's is a special situation of "treble solitude": "of the sea, the neighboring island, and the ship" (*IDB* 3-4).

Initially Roberto wants to reach the island which he can see from the ship, but cannot access. What is it like? What things are there? Or is it just an illusion like some charming but unreal mirage? Roberto della Griva, the young outcast, knows it is 'the island of the day before', and accordingly, if he could swim across, he would have been able to change his fate. The distant view of the island continues to fascinate him; it is 'marvellous', but not 'possession' (*à la* Greenblatt). Roberto gets captivated by the distant island (*IDB* 276), which invites him with the lure of the 'virgin land'. Roberto in his isolation on board speculates: "How would the island seem to him if he were to reach one day.... Was it perhaps the Eden where milk and honey flow in streams, amid abundant trophies of fruit and flocks of meek animals? ...a Terra Incognita that would finally renew the offerings of a vale untainted by the sin of Babel or by the Flood or by Adam's Fall?....

But if this was so, would he not be repeating the error of the first sinner if he chose to violate the virginity of the island? Perhaps Providence had rightly wanted him to be a chaste witness to a beauty that he should never disturb" (*IDB* 104).

Roberto's fascination and obsession with 'islands', a characteristic feature of the age, is evidenced by his dream-visions as well in which he envisions various real, surreal, hyperreal islands. Again, the course of Roberto's 'dream' or imagination also follows the paths as laid out by the fantastic travel-tales of his times. Indeed the narration itself pertains of the quality of a wry dream (fragmentary too, like Kubla Khan's!): Roberto imagines/dreams sea voyages and arrival at islands from "infinite parallaxes" (441; 442-48): the fantasy island in the Pacific (442); grotesque island (442); horrid nightmarish islands (442-43); the Island of Invisible Men (443); island of the Fount of Youth (444). Roberto dreams of metafictional islands too; the islanders (of the 6th island of Roberto's dream) who could live only if narrated (444);

On the one hand the textuality of the 'desert island' is emphasized. At the same time, on the other hand, the narration, which often reverts to an interior monologue, takes wings to the dream-region of the romantics. By means of a superb feat of imaginative flight the dream-element of the situation has been reinforced.

> ...he had often asked himself if he was not dreaming. What was happening to him did not usually happen to humans; at best it evoked the novels of childhood. Like dream-creatures were the ship and the animals he had encountered on it; of the same substance as dreams were the shadows that for three days had enfolded him.... Could not, then, the great theater of celestial crew, which he now thought he saw on the horizon, be likewise a dream? (*IDB* 64-65)

This may be seen in connection with/in the light of Pedro Calderon's (1600-81) theory, which held the day in Spain around the time that 'this life's a dream'.

While remaining physically stagnated on the anchored ship Roberto makes his dream-voyage, following his imaginary double, Ferrante, on his voyage. Before setting on the pursuit he persuades himself, that the world could be experienced from "infinite parallaxes" (*IDB* 441). It is a fantasy voyage, almost Odyssean in its play of imagination, where the voyagers meet sea-monsters as well as a host of similar miraculous phenomena. He visits in dream seven such islands, some beautiful, some hideous, some terrifying, some alluring, in quick and smooth succession (*IDB* 442-47), which is possible and ensured only in dream.

That this island is supposed to belong to empirical reality, and yet to embrace the domain of hyperreality, is a further reason for its unreachability as well as its attraction.

The hyperreality of the specific oxymoronic island of Roberto, with its 'distant proximity', is accentuated by the dream-tenor of the narrative as well as by covert/and overt mythical allusions, which have been lying strewn about unmistakably. For instance, the evocation of the Lotos-Eators: "The only reality of the Island was that in its center stood, tempting in delicate hues, the Tree of Oblivion, whose fruit, if Roberto ate it, could give him peace.... To disremember…" (*IDB* 105).

Other mythic evocations include Aeneas, holding the golden bough, and descending into the Hades (*IDB* 353); the doves of The Greek and Biblical myths (353); Adonis myth in the 4th island of Roberto's dream (*IDB* 444); Narcissus myth in the 5th island of Roberto's dream (*IDB* 444); Neptune (*IDB* 484); the Biblical allusion to the dove (*IDB* 279); Roberto's dream-visions of various islands (*IDB* 442-48) are finally clinched with the 'dove': "on an almond tree bejewelled with blossoms lamented the Orange Dove…" (*IDB* 448; 344; 347); Christ & the Orange Dove (*IDB* 459). The book ends with the vision of the orange Dove,—Roberto's anticipation to "see rising in flight—like an arrow eager to strike the sun—the Orange Dove" (*IDB* 503; 508). Roberto wonders: "Was he seeing them because he had truly been shipwrecked at the edge of the Garden of Eden, or was it because he had emerged from the belly of the ship as from a hellish funnel? Both perhaps…" (*IDB* 108).

The reader can identify many such Biblical echoes which are in tune with the time-frame of the story: for instance, myth of Jonah (*IDB* 447), Flame Dove and the Solomon Island (*IDB* 177), etc.

Apart from this Eco takes up one of the most trendy and urgent preoccupations of the times, regarding the search for the Biblical location of the Islands of Solomon (*IDB* 244). It is about the famous 'Longitude Problem', and the attempt of the European nations at the time to discover longitude. Longitude is the motif of the novel, and search for it the motive behind the action. "The great mystery of the tides mattered far less to him than the great mystery of that line, beyond which Time went backwards" (*IDB* 298).

The search is simultaneously about the Island of Solomon and the longitude, the hundred-eightieth meridian. The theological notion and the [pseudo] scientific concepts seem to be interchangeable variables. It is the 'terra incognita'.

Roberto asks Caspar: "were you hunting for the Islands of Solomon or did you want to solve the mystery of longitudes?"

"Why, both, is it not? You find the Islands of Solomon and you have learned where is the hundred-eightieth meridian, you find the hundred-eightieth meridian and you know where are the Islands of Solomon!" (252-53); also see (260); "...at this point of the earth there is a line that on this side is the day after and on that side the day before..." (*IDB* 266). Roberto opts for the antipode island (*IDB* 340), and his brain-child Ferrento orders to set sail for the islands of Solomon. (*IDB* 440)

Apparently the allusion is to antipodal meridian which today we call the International Date Line. At the same time, Eco presents a fantasy island in the garb of mystic knowledge disseminated by a supposedly medieval theologian-cum-scientist who subverts the basic tenets of Crucifixion and Redemption. Ferrante, the alter ego of Roberto, claims to have gone on the far side of the island of Solomon, and hijacked Christ from Calvary:

> "...sailed through my long Thursday towards Jerusalem, found the other Judas on the verge of betraying, hanged him from tree, preventing him from handing over the Son of Man to the Sons of Darkness, entered the Garden of Olives with my men and abducted Our Lord, stealing Him from Calvary! And now you, I, all of us are living in a world which has never been redeemed!"
>
> "But where Christ now?"...
>
> "Do you then not know that the ancient texts already said there are doves the color of flame because the Lord, before being crucified, wore a scarlet tunic? Have you not yet understood? For one thousand

> six hundred and ten years Christ has been prisoner on this Island, whence He tries to escape in the form of an Orange Dove, but is unable to abandon that place, where next to the Specula Melitensis I have left Judas's scapular, and where it is therefore forever the same day." (*IDB* 459)

At one level it is about 'the Island not found', not findable, and, paradoxically, about the protagonist's voyage for the same. How could one reach the unreachable! And yet, who knows! The ironical allusion to Othello's famous speech seems to quiver with the weight of signification: "…ignorance of the fisherman of the Island Not Found who, beyond the last horizon of the Canaries, foolishly discards the rarest among pearls…" (*IDB* 130).

And in the meantime, how can he ignore/withstand the great attraction of the 'Island'! He uses the spyglass he had found in the adjoining cabin, and gazes at the farthest corner of the bay. "The island seemed pale, its peak tufted with a patch of wool. As he had learned on the *Amaralis*, ocean islands retain the humidity of the Trades and condense it in cloudy puffs, so that sailors often recognize the presence of land before they can see the shores, from the clumps of the airy element that it holds as if they were anchored there" (100).

His yearning for the island, so close, yet so inaccessible, grows,

While on board of the *Daphne* Roberto comes across some island maps. "Some cartographers, to make an island recognizable, simply drew with great precision the form of the peaks…. Late in the night we find Roberto daydreaming over the map now transformed into the desired female body…. The map repeated many times the features of that beloved body, in various attitudes of bays and promontories" (129). However, he will be denied the possession of both. The attraction of the 'Island' is further enhanced by the inaccessible proximity; it is so close yet so far. The attraction of the unaccessed 'Island' for Roberto's mind is accentuated through the equation between the spit of land and his beloved. The first time Roberto realized that he was inside the "wooden womb" of a "floating house" (*IDB* 100), "he thought of the island and defined it as unattainable proximity" (*IDB* 100); this leads him further to conjecture on the comparability of the island with his 'Lady', a thought that thrills his mind. "This fine conceit showed him, for the second time that day, the dissimilar similitude between the island and the Lady, and he stayed awake into the night to pen the pages I have drawn on for this chapter"

(*IDB* 100). Then it becomes the epitome also for his eluding beloved, thus obliquely suggesting an equation between the island and the elusive love: both the lady and the island remain equally inaccessible.

> "the wreck had granted him the supreme gift, exile, and a Lady whom no one could now take from him....
>
> But the island did not belong to him and remained distant. *The Daphne* did not belong to him...." (*IDB* 227)

Thus he becomes the 'no-where-man' in the very modern sense of the term.

Like all works of Eco, this book too is frankly cerebrative. And like Eco again, it is so many things at the same time. Bob Corbett remarks: "Roberto is, in a sense an everyman—not, however a commoner, but reasonably educated and privileged (as are most of Eco's readers) who is used to weaving an entertaining story of how such a 17th century man would understand and explore the world."

It is indeed a period piece, but it is so in more senses than one, embracing and incorporating alongside material detail, various philosophical, metaphysical, scientific (including astronomy and physics), and theological discourses of the time and place, i.e., Europe in the early 17th century. The continuum is not unfamiliar to the readers of Eco's fiction. The author as is usual with him, seems to be almost juggling, with as much skill as enjoyment, between these varied ideas and discourses. And the playfulness of the act of juggling bubbles up at various turns of the narrative, which is again dished out as the result of an 'editing' of the notebook of Roberto, done by a later-day ephebe, obviously Eco himself.

However, one cannot but acknowledge that in spite of the crowded ideas, obscure references and antique time-space continuum the book exerts its own charm upon the reader. Some of the perennial themes addressed here are love, life, death, 'Time' and God,—and the island, which is so near, yet remains so far, serves as the pivotal point of this revolving, multi-modal mirror.

Another theme that runs parallel all along is self-discovery, a kind of mental journey toward an innermost island through the tides of Time. As Roberto tries to swim across, the 'Island' seems to be receding. Eventually he sees it "distant not only in space, but also (backwards) in time" (*IDB* 362). After a few days he abandons all attempts at swimming and "thinks once more of an Island made to his measure, or, rather, to the measure of his dreams" (*IDB* 362).

At one point, in his extreme frustration Roberto tries to conquer time by means of throwing away all the clocks on the ship, proclaiming the fascination of time, but in his case the doom awaiting. The storeroom of the Daphne contains all sorts of clocks—water clocks, sand clocks, solar clocks, mechanical clocks (*IDB* 149-50): "Imagine a castaway, amid the fumes of aqua vitae, on an uninhabited vessel, finding a hundred clocks almost all in unison telling the tale of his interminable time…a man sentenced to a very long death" (150). At the end "he flung into the sea all the clocks, not thinking for a moment that he was wasting valuable time: he was erasing time to favor a journey against time" (*IDB* 502).

Towards the end Roberto realizes the inescapability of his situation,—that he should "never wander", neither towards the island, nor towards the outer sea; but this brings a strange feeling of freedom/peace attained through speculations about being and nothingness. He thinks of the mystery of death and the greater mystery of life, of the beginning. And he comes to the conclusion: "This was why he had been cast up on the Daphne.... Because only in that restful hermitage would he have had the leisure to reflect on the one question that frees us from every apprehension about not being and consigns us to the wonder of being" (468). So he gives up worrying over not finding the unfindable, not reaching the island that cannot be reached.

For opposite and conflicting reasons he thinks it positively undesirable for a time. Firstly, if it is a place inhabited by innocent pure people who know no avarice, then why should one taint it with the sin of greed? Secondly, if it were to be equated with his Lady, then was it not his duty to prevent intrusion from outside, to forestall violation of the "virginity of the Island" (104)? "And to that same chastity he must feel bound with regard to the Island: the more he wished it to be rich in promises, the less he should want to touch it. Far from the Lady, far from the Island, he should only speak of them, wanting them immaculate as long as they could keep..., touched only by the caress of the elements. If there was beauty somewhere, its purpose was to remain purposeless" (*IDB* 105).

But he is not sure if he has been right in his guess; it may be terrible as well; it might have been holding terrible people; and that too offered sufficient ground for withdrawal: "Was the island he saw really like that?... It was known that from the time of the first voyages to these islands, situated vaguely on the maps, mutineers were abandoned there, and the islands became prisons with bars of air, in which the condemned were their own jailers, punishing one another reciprocally. Not to arrive there, not to discover the secret was, more than a duty, a reprieve from endless horrors" (*IDB* 105).

However, finally a time comes when Roberto takes his final plunge: after freeing the birds, and throwing away all the clocks, "because he was erasing time to favor a journey against time" (502), "he descended into the sea" (503).

> "Before destiny, and the waters, decide for him, I hope that—pausing for breath every so often—he allows his eyes to move from the Daphne, as he bids it farewell, to the Island.
>
> There, above the line traced by the treetops, his eyes now very sharp, he should see rising in flight—like an arrow eager to strike the sun—the Orange Dove." (503)

Is it the phoenix, or the Resurrected Son of God?

Anyway, by this act of 'descending' he loses his foothold,—the mini-island of the ship perpetually. But does he reach the 'Island'? One cannot tell. Who knows? Now he is in no position to leave diary-notes any more, and the reader is left only to guess about this postmodern Odysseus who has no home, no kin, no land to rest his feet upon, no mission (which has been lost in course of the voyage, and finally no destination.

WORKS CITED

Becket, Fiona. *The Complete Critical Guide to D.H. Lawrence*. London and NY: Routledge, 2002.

Brewster, Dorothy. *Virginia Woolf.* (1962). London: George Allen & Unwin Ltd., 1963.

Corbett, Bob., 'Comments' November 2004. http://www. webster.edu/~corbetre/personal/reading/eco-island.html corbetre@webster.edu

Coroneos, Con and Trudi Tate. 'Lawrence's Tales'. *The Cambridge Companion to D.H. Lawrence.* [Ed.] Anne Fernihough. Cambridge: CUP, 2001.

Daiches, David. 'Symbolic Pattern in *To the Lighthouse*', *Critics on Virginia Woolf* Latham, E.M. [ed.]. London: George Allen & Unwin Ltd., 1970), 70-71.

Eco, Umberto. *The Island of the Day Before*. (trans. from the Italian by William Weaver). London: Vintage, 1998.

Ellis, David. *D.H. Lawrence: Dying Game 1922–1930*. Cambridge: Cambridge University Press, 1998.

Franks, Jill. "To make a world of his own": Psychoanalysis and Weltanschauung in 'The Man Who Loved Islands'. *D.H. Lawrence Studies* 15.2 (August 2007). Eds. Michael Bell, Chong-wha Chung, Virginia Hyde and Nak-chung Paik. Seoul: The D.H. Lawrence Society of Korea. 147-57.

Gordon, Lyndall. 'A Writer's Life', in Eric Warner [ed.] *Virginia Woolf: A Centenary Perspective*. 56-68.

Graham, John. 'Time in the Novels of Virginia Woolf,' *Critics on Virginia Woolf.* Latham, E.M. [ed.]. London: George Allen & Unwin Ltd., 1970), 28-44.

Green, Jared F. 'The Semiotics of Motherhood'. In Merli, 123-42.

Merli, Carol [ed.] *Illuminations: New Readings of Virginia Woolf.* New Delhi: Macmillan India Ltd., 2004.

Schaefer, Josephine O'Brien. 'Mr and Mrs Ramsay', *Critics on Virginia Woolf.* Latham, E.M. [ed.]. London: George Allen & Unwin Ltd., 1970), 70-78.

Lawrence, D.H. 'The Man who Loved Islands'. *Love Among the Haystacks and Other Stories.* (1930). Harmondsworth: Penguin Books, 1968.

Simon, Irene. 'The Sea in *To the Lighthouse*', *Critics on Virginia Woolf.* Latham, E.M. [ed.]. London: George Allen & Unwin Ltd., 1970), 79-81.

Stoltzfus, Ben. "'The Man Who Loved Islands': A Lacanian Reading." *D.H. Lawrence Review* 29.3 (2000): 27-38.

Turner, John F. "The Capacity to be Alone and Its Failure in D.H. Lawrence's 'The Man Who Loved Islands.'" *D.H. Lawrence Review* 16.3 (1983): 259-89.

Warner, Eric [ed.]. *Virginia Woolf: A Centenary Perspective*. London: The Macmillan Press Ltd., 1984; rpt. 1988.

Wilson, Gregory. 'Temporal Vision: Modernism and Time in *To the Lighthouse*'. In Merli. 73-86.

Willbern, David. "Malice in Paradise: Isolation and Projection in 'The Man Who Loved Islands,'" *D.H. Lawrence Review* 10 (1977): 223-41.

❑❑❑

List contd. on next page

52. WILLIAM GOLDING: CRITICAL STUDIES
53. MARK TWAIN: CRITICAL STUDIES
54. HERMAN MELVILLE: CRITICAL STUDIES
55. LEWIS CARROLL: CRITICAL STUDIES
56. MATTHEW ARNOLD: CRITICAL STUDIES
57. RICHARD WRIGHT: CRITICAL STUDIES
58. RUDYARD KIPLING: CRITICAL STUDIES
59. WILLIAM FAULKNER: CRITICAL STUDIES
60. SAUL BELLOW: CRITICAL STUDIES
61. EUGENE O'NEILL: CRITICAL STUDIES
62. KATHERINE MANSFIELD: CRITICAL STUDIES
63. TENESSEE WILLIAMS: CRITICAL STUDIES
64. NATHANIEL HAWTHORNE: CRITICAL STUDIES
65. PHILIP LARKIN: CRITICAL STUDIES
66. TED HUGHES: CRITICAL STUDIES
67. STEPHEN SPENDER: CRITICAL STUDIES
68. SRI AUROBINDO: CRITICAL STUDIES
69. SAROJINI NAIDU: CRITICAL STUDIES
70. MULK RAJ ANAND: CRITICAL STUDIES
71. R.K. NARAYAN: CRITICAL STUDIES
72. RAJA RAO: CRITICAL STUDIES
73. ANITA DESAI: CRITICAL STUDIES
74. AMITAV GHOSH: CRITICAL STUDIES
75. SALMAN RUSHDIE: CRITICAL STUDIES
76. GITHA HARIHARAN: CRITICAL STUDIES
77. SHASHI THAROOR: CRITICAL STUDIES
78. CHINUA ACHEBE: CRITICAL STUDIES
79. WOLE SOYINKA: CRITICAL STUDIES
80. JEAN RHYS: CRITICAL STUDIES
81. MARGARET ATWOOD: CRITICAL STUDIES
82. TONI MORRISON: CRITICAL STUDIES
83. ALICE WALKER: CRITICAL STUDIES
84. JAMAICA KINCAID: CRITICAL STUDIES
85. DEREK WALCOTT: CRITICAL STUDIES
86. CARYL PHILLIPS: CRITICAL STUDIES
87. HANIF KUREISHI: CRITICAL STUDIES
88. DORIS LESSING: CRITICAL STUDIES
89. JOHN FOWLES: CRITICAL STUDIES
90. CARYL CHURCH: CRITICAL STUDIES
91. VIJAY TENDULKAR: CRITICAL STUDIES
92. GABRIEL GARCIA MARQUEZ: CRITICAL STUDIES
93. MILAN KUNDERA: CRITICAL STUDIES
94. J.L. BORGES: CRITICAL STUDIES
95. NADINE GORDIMER: CRITICAL STUDIES
96. J.M. COETZEE: CRITICAL STUDIES
97. GIRISH KARNAD: CRITICAL STUDIES
98. PATRICK WHITE: CRITICAL STUDIES
99. BERTOLT BRECHT: CRITICAL STUDIES
100. HEINRICH IBSEN: CRITICAL STUDIES
101. LEO TOLSTOY: CRITICAL STUDIES
102. ALBERT CAMUS: CRITICAL STUDIES
103. FRANZ KAFKA: CRITICAL STUDIES
104. GUNTER GRASS: CRITICAL STUDIES

The papers must be critical, analytical and comprehensive and not of journalistic nature. There is no limit on the length of papers; papers of any length would be included in full. Papers containing typographical or language errors would not be considered. Papers already published elsewhere are also accepted if they are free from copyright problems. Similarly, papers presented at conferences, seminars, etc. are also welcome.

We will send a complementary copy of the volume to all contributors offering papers of not less than ten printed pages.

Please let us know if you or any of your colleagues are interested in sending papers for publication in the aforementioned volumes.

We will appreciate it very much if you share this information with your friends and colleagues.